A Dictionary of
Monsters and Mysterious Beasts

CW00733672

A Dictionary of Monsters and Mysterious Beasts

Revised edition

Carey Miller

Illustrated by Mary I. French

A Piccolo Original
Piccolo Books

First published 1974 by Pan Books Ltd,
This revised and extended edition
published 1987 by Pan Books Ltd
Cavaye Place London SW10 9PG
Text © Carey Miller 1974, 1987
Illustrations © Mary I. French 1974, 1987
ISBN 0 330 296701
10 9 8 7 6 5 4 3 2 1
Printed and bound in Great Britain by
Cox & Wyman Ltd, Reading

This book is sold subject to the condition that it
shall not, by way of trade or otherwise, be lent, re-sold,
hired out or otherwise circulated without the publisher's prior
consent in any form of binding or cover other than that in which
it is published and without a similar condition including this
condition being imposed on the subsequent purchaser.

'Monster' comes from the Latin word monstrum, *meaning 'omen', for the appearance of strange and sinister creatures was thought to herald unusual and disturbing events.*

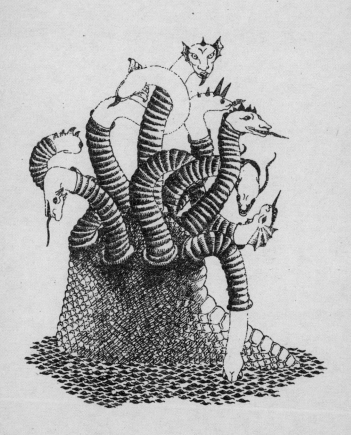

To Sybil and Stanley, with all my love
(*Carey Miller's Dedication*)

Message from the author

We all love monsters – from the child who imagines weird and wonderful creatures lurking in the shadows of his bedroom to the adult who spends money to sit in a darkened cinema to be terrified by the man-made monster on the screen. It's a strange fact, but at some time or another we all enjoy being frightened. To some it is merely being hurled around too fast on a fairground ride that makes us scream with fearful delight, but to most of us the prospect of a strange, unknown creature is endlessly fascinating. Particularly if we are unlikely to meet it face to face! This enjoyment of fear was probably not common to the people of earliest civilizations and it is easy to understand how their fears started – groups of primitive people huddling around small flickering fires and surrounded by a great darkness and a lot of eerie inexplicable noises. If you thought about it – and at that time of night there was little else to think about – there could be absolutely anything out there just waiting for the right moment to come and snatch you away!

Perhaps there really were gigantic, scaly, fire-breathing, two-headed monsters out there, perhaps the dead could come to life and haunt the living, maybe the sea *was* full of evil, writhing things just waiting to drag you under. Who could say? The tales they told each other to explain away their fears were passed down from generation to generation. If someone told you today that they had seen a Hippogriff in the High Street or that their Auntie May had been swallowed by a Kraken whilst paddling, you would probably be very amused. Certainly you would not take it seriously even for a second. Yet it was no joke to primitive man – these sort of occurrences seemed highly likely!

When people were able to travel from one country to another they brought home even more amazing tales of creatures who lived in foreign lands. Apparently, in these faraway, mysterious places there were creatures like gigantic lizards with glittering, needle-sharp teeth and jaws that could break a man in two (crocodiles); and wild-eyed cat-like creatures, but a hundred times bigger with vicious teeth and claws that could tear you apart before you could shout 'Help!' (tigers); and serpents as wide as the trunk of a tree that could swallow a whole cow without difficulty (pythons). When these stories were embroidered a little here and there they were enough to scare anybody who had not actually seen the creatures out of their wits!

Many of the monsters in this book are based on real animals with human exaggerations making them quite unrecognizable. For instance, could the Kraken or the Hai Ho Shang really have been a sort of giant squid? It's quite possible. Other sorts of monsters could be totally imaginary beings invented by frightened humans to explain away natural things that they didn't understand, like storms and earthquakes.

On the other hand, it is only recently, probably within the last fifty years, that it has become fashionable to dismiss

monster sightings as the evidence of easily frightened people misrepresenting clues, or as intentional or unintentional hoaxes. Can this be the explanation of one hundred per cent of all monster reports, or does it, perhaps, account for only ninety-eight per cent of them? If so, what about the other two per cent?

In the latest edition of this book I have discovered several new monsters and more spine-chilling evidence on the old ones. Afterwards readers may well decide that it is better to be an armchair participant than an eye-witness when it comes to monster-hunting. If you do decide to hunt, begin with the shelves of your library or bookshop, looking first in the Folk Tales section. And always remember to check under your bed before you get into it. Don't bother to lock your bedroom door, though – the monsters that aren't strong enough to break it down will probably ooze in through the keyhole!

C. M.

The Abominable Snowman or Yeti

For the last two thousand years in various corners of the world there have been continuous reports of a wild, shaggy beast that walks upright like a man. This hairy monster comes under many different names. The American Indians call it Sasquatch (see page 114), Wauk Wauk or Ice Giant; in Africa it is called the Nandi Bear (see page 101) or the Chemosit, in Tibet the Mi-gö or the Yeti, in Mongolia the Almas, in China the Hsileh-Jen, in Russia the Almast. In England we call it the Bigfoot or the Abominable Snowman.

Probably the best-known of these mysterious creatures – in the Western world at least – is the Himalayan version called the Yeti. The remarkable thing about this animal is that the natives of the different countries spanned by the Himalayas – the Tibetans, the Sherpas and the Lepchas – all give identical descriptions of the creature. Tibet's most 'wanted' man is apparently about 2 metres (between 7 and 7½ feet) tall when standing erect. He has a powerful body completely covered with brown hair, and long arms. He has an oval head, pointed at the top, with an ape-like face. In spite of his great strength, he is regarded by most of the inhabitants of the Himalayas as a harmless creature who would attack a human only if he were wounded.

According to the native hunters the name 'snowman' is not an appropriate one, for this odd creature is not really human at all, and, instead of living in the snowy regions, he has his lair in the thick forests high on the slopes of the Himalayas where he sleeps all day and leaves his den only under cover of darkness. His approach is heralded by the crackling of branches and an eerie whistling cry. In the forest he moves on all fours or by swinging from trees, but in open country he is said to walk upright with a sort of shambling roll rather like a sailor. It must be a tiring, miserable journey for the Yeti to climb up to the desolate snowlands. He does this, apparently, because he likes a particular sort of salty moss (said to be rich in vitamins) that grows on rocks in the snowfields. When he has taken as much as he needs he returns to the forest, leaving his gigantic footprints in the snow.

These legends of the Yeti are centuries old in the regions of the Himalayas, but the people of the Western world came to hear about the creature only in 1921. This was the year when a British mountaineer, Howard Bury, led an expedition to scale Mount Everest, the highest mountain in the world. Although he was a very experienced climber and familiar with the border country between India and Tibet, the expedition was not a success. The news of Colonel Bury's failure, however, was soon overshadowed by the strange discovery the party made during their climb. Apparently they had

Yeti footprint

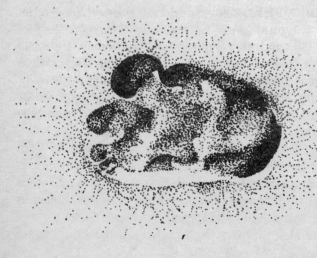

found large sets of what appeared to be human footprints in the snow! The local people hired to go on the trip with them told Bury that they were the tracks of the wild, hairy men who inhabited the most remote mountain areas. This amazing news spread through the Western world like wildfire and it soon became the obsession of every explorer to capture a 'snowman' of his own.

Endless tales were told by the natives of the many times they had seen the Yeti, and at least two were said to have been captured and brought down the mountain. One of them, an adult male, was tied hand and foot for his long journey down the mountain but, unfortunately, he was upset and frightened and refused to eat. Before the journey was over he became very weak and died. His captors, not realizing the significance of their discovery, threw the poor creature's body away! In spite of all the natives' tales, Western people found the story of the Abominable Snowman difficult to swallow. No English-speaking witness had come forward, and in any case no creature could possibly exist at those heights – what would he use for food? The story of the Abominable Snowman became a nine-days' wonder – an amusing joke that no one took seriously!

Then in 1951 a British explorer, Eric Shipton, scouting for an alternative route to climb Everest, found another long set of tracks. He and his party were 6,960 kilometres (19,000 feet) above sea level and crossing a treacherous glacier when they spotted the footprints. They appeared to be made by an upright, two-footed animal with gigantic feet. Fortunately, Shipton had a camera with him and was able to get some very clear photographs. The mysterious 'thing' seemed to have passed over almost impossible obstacles that would have proved difficult even for an experienced climber using all the tools of his trade. The huge prints also clearly showed that, where the animal had jumped across a wide crevasse in the glacier, it had dug its toes in deeply to prevent itself from falling.

The photographs were published in the *Illustrated London News* and created a furore. Suddenly, everyone believed in the Snowman all over again except, of course, the scientists, who said it couldn't possibly exist! Eric Shipton was certainly convinced of its existence and so was his colleague Edmund Hillary, the mountaineer who became famous as the man who conquered the world's greatest peak on the successful Everest expedition of 1953. Seven years after Hillary had fulfilled his life's ambition and been knighted by the Queen, he returned to Everest in the hope of fulfilling another ambition, that of capturing a real live Yeti and bringing it down the mountain. The main purpose of Hillary's party was to climb the Himalayas as high as 6,960 kilometres in order to try and live there for six months. It was really an experiment to test the reactions of the human body to life at this altitude for long periods. Yet all the time the expedition was on the lookout for the Yeti. Many sets of footprints were found, but not once did they catch a glimpse of the elusive Yeti itself. The party did, however, bring back what were claimed to be two Yeti scalps, loaned to them by a Nepalese monastery which had had them as long as anyone could remember. When the scalps were examined by experts in London, Paris and Chicago they were found to be very old indeed but quite obvious fakes, probably made from the skin of a long-haired goat. Hillary was by now beginning to have serious doubts about the Snowman's existence and so were the press, who were quick to publish the results, or lack of results, of the expedition.

However, in 1964, just as the interest once again died down in the West, a Russian scientist, Boris Porshnev, announced that he had also been investigating the Snowman and was now convinced that the Yeti was a survivor of the prehistoric men that lived in Europe as long as 75,000 years ago. He refused to give out any further details of his secret findings. Other important Russian scientists also came forward in agreement; Professor A.G. Pronin even claimed to have seen a Yeti on two separate occasions.

In the spring of 1966 a man named Didanov, highly respected in his village in the Caucasus Mountains, told of his personal experience with a strange hairy animal. Didanov was travelling through the mountain pastures when he received an invitation to have supper and spend the night at a shepherds' encampment. Unfortunately Didanov had problems getting off to sleep because of the restlessness of the man lying next to him in the large tent. Didanov had just rolled over when he saw a large hand parting the tent flaps. According to the terrified traveller (reported in the magazine *Nauka i Religiya*) a 'hairy thing' entered. Didanov screwed up his eyes and feigned sleep but watched everything that happened, even though he was scared stiff.

After a wary glance around the tent the unknown creature squatted down beside the food supplies and proceeded to remove the lids from large containers. It then gobbled up vast quantities of food before replacing the container lids and slipping silently out of the tent. The next morning Didanov pointed out the depleted food supplies to his host and described his visitor. 'Pay no attention,' said his host, smiling. 'You will see a lot more than that if you stay in this area for long. It is only what we call an Almasti.'

Igor Tatsl, a Soviet mountaineer, said in August 1981 that he and his fellow-climbers had seen an Abominable Snowman at close quarters. As proof Tatsl had taken an imprint of the creature's foot, clearly seen in the mud on a tributary of the Varzog River.

'We are aiming at friendly spontaneous contact,' said Tatsl. 'I don't think it is possible to capture the creature but we hope to make friends with it.'

The Two-Headed Amphisbaena

An Amphisbaena is a two-headed reptilian creature that can move both forwards and backwards. When one head slept, the other head stayed awake to keep watch. In early church sculpture it is usually shown as a Dragon with a second head growing from its tail. These creatures can still be seen in churches built between the twelfth and fifteenth centuries, sometimes carved in the stonework on fonts but more often as the wooden carvings on the undersides of choir seats, known as misericords. There is a particulary interesting Amphisbaena on one of the stone knobs or bosses on the old nave roof of Southwark Cathedral in London. This carving is of the Dragon variety with large wings and almost identical heads. Pliny, a Roman writer living in the first century AD, who seems to know a lot about it, tells us that the best remedy for a cold is to wrap a dead Amphisbaena (or its skin) around one's body. He also informs us that if a dead Amphisbaena is nailed to a tree about to be felled the woodcutter will never feel the cold and will fell the tree more easily. Other information tells us that it can run with lightning speed, its eyes burn like candles and it lives on ants. Apparently if it is chopped in half its two parts will join together again and it will be fit and healthy!

Amphisbaena

The Banshee

No one has ever come forward with evidence concerning the shape of the Banshee and, as far as we know, she has none. She is just a screaming, wailing voice that haunts the Irish night and disturbs the sleep of the Scottish Highlanders. Her mournful cry, or keening, has also been heard in Wales and in Brittany and, if heard outside the house at night, it foretells a death in the family. When her wail is low and sweet, an omen of gentle death can be interpreted. When the sound is angry and strident, death will be gruesome and violent.

The Basilisk (Cockatrice)

It was a firm belief in the fifteenth century that elderly cocks could lay eggs, and one poor creature was actually brought to trial in the public courts and found guilty of having done just that! These unfortunate fowls were said to lay their eggs in a warm dungheap or give them over to a toad or a snake to hatch. The end product was always the same and struck dread in the heart of all who heard its name – the Basilisk!

The Basilisk's breath was poisonous and withered all vegetation except the rue (an evergreen shrub). Its glance was fatal to all men and animals, apart from the weasel, and shattered giant rocks into splinters. If, by any remote chance, a blind person with no sense of smell managed to kill a Basilisk, its deadly venom would travel through the weapon and strike dead the person who held it. The Basilisk was quite small, under 60 centimetres (2 feet) in length, and had a crusty yellow and black skin. It had pointed wings and a yellow tail that curled over its back like a scorpion's. Its eyes were toad-like and fiery-red and its head was thought to be that of a cock, or sometimes a snake wearing a pointed coxcomb rather like a crown. It was known as the King of Serpents and took its name from the Greek word *basilisk* meaning 'King'. It was certainly monarch of the reptile world and its hissing approach caused all other snakes to flee.

The Basilisk lived in warm climates, usually in deserts of its own creation. Any stream that quenched its thirst was poisoned for centuries and its glance burnt up the grass for miles around. There were only two things it feared, the weasel and the sound of a crowing cock. Any unfortunate traveller needing to cross a desert was always careful to take with him a weasel or a rooster in a cage.

There was one other deadly weapon in the fight against the Basilisk, and that was a mirror. If a mirror could be held up before it, it would look into it and immediately fall dead. It was also said during the fifteenth century that England was so infested with Basilisks that no man dared to leave his own

Basilisk (Cockatrice)

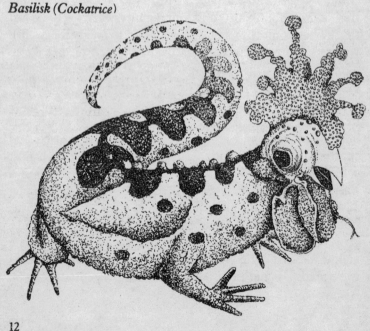

front door. Eventually, a brave man came forward in a bid to rid the country of this evil plague. He encased himself in a suit made entirely from mirrors and walked back and forth from one end of the country to the other, until not one Basilisk remained alive.

The last reported appearence of a really nasty Basilisk was said to be in 1587 in Warsaw. Two little girls playing in a derelict old house found a set of steps leading down into a cellar. They ran down them and were met with such poisonous air that they both fell dead on the spot. When they were missed their nurse followed them down the steps and suffered the same horrible fate. Rumours soon began to circulate around the city until they came to the ears of the King's wise old doctor. He knew at once that the cellar must be occupied by a Basilisk and ordered that a man in a mirrored suit should be sent down at once. Needless to say, there was no rush of volunteers for this exciting mission, but eventually a condemned criminal was persuaded to offer his services. He was given a lighted torch and a rake and sent down the steps. A crowd of two thousand gathered to watch him. After some time he reappeared, carrying the body of a disappointingly small snake. The doctor declared at once that it was certainly a Basilisk, and no one dared to disagree! Afterwards, belief in this particular breed of monster began to die out and today it exists only as a small harmless lizard in South America which certainly bears little resemblance to its hideous and mythical ancestor.

The Berbalangs of Cagayan Sulu

Cagayan Sulu is a tiny island on the southern edge of the Philippine Islands, set in the Pacific Ocean near Malaysia. It was visited in the 1890s by a Mr Ethelbert Forbes Sketchley of Hong Kong, who, as a result of what he found there, wrote an article which was then published in a very respectable newspaper – the *Journal of the Asiatic Society of Bengal* – in 1896. It was called 'Cagayan Sulu, its Customs, Legends and Superstitions', and it was filled with the most amazing information.

It tells of a tiny village in the middle of the island of Cagayan Sulu that is inhabited by a group of fearsome ghouls called Berbalangs. The Berbalangs were said to have wings and cat-like slits for eyes, but, in every other way, they looked like normal human beings. They need human flesh in order to live and spend their time digging into graves and eating the bodies that they find there. When the supply of corpses in Cagayan Sulu is scarce the Berbalangs make a hiding-place in the grass, and by lying down and holding their breath can put themselves into a trance. Their invisible astral body then leaves the sleeping one and goes off to find food instead. Apparently, the Berbalangs can alway be heard approaching, as they make a loud moaning noise that fades to a feeble groan as they arrive. Their eyes can also be observed at a distance, for they sparkle and dance like fire-flies.

According to Mr Sketchley, you are safe from attack only if you carry a coconut pearl, a stone like an opal. Should you be caught without one, you can attempt to beat off the Berbalangs with a kris (a dagger with a wavy blade) rubbed with the juice of a lime. If you hear the ghoul moaning in front of you and see the flashing lights of his eyes, turn round suddenly and start slashing behind you, for Berbalangs are always contrary and are never where they seem to be!

The graves in Cagayan Sulu are built under or near the houses of the people, so that they can be sprinkled daily with fresh lime juice to keep the Berbalangs from devouring the contents.

Most of what Mr Sketchley wrote in his article is the truth about the Berbalangs as described by the people of Cagayan Sulu, who were really very afraid of them in the way some Europeans were terrified of Vampires during the same period. In fact, Berbalangs, Werewolves and Vampires have a lot in common and could easily have been cousins. If you accept this, it is easy to dismiss the Berbalangs as part of a universal folklore; however, Mr Sketchley does not do this and goes on to tell of his own meeting with a pack of Berbalangs who walked down the valley towards him one day when he lay hidden in the grass. He said that the experience gave him 'a very creepy sensation about the roots of his hair'. He goes on to say that he found an acquaintance of his, Hassan, lying dead of fright but uneaten after a visit from the Berbalangs! I can't explain Mr Sketchley's story, can you?

Bishop-Fish and Monk-Fish

In the Middle Ages there was a curious belief that everything in the air or on the earth had its double in the sea. So when a previously undiscovered fish was found washed up off the coast of Norway and described as having a close-shaven head and an ungracious face, it was straightaway christened Monk-Fish. Its shoulders were said to be covered with what appeared to be a monk's hood with feathering fins for arms, and a long tail at the end of its body. The King of Poland took a particular interest in this odd fish, and asked for it to be sent for him to see.

When it was presented at Court it made known to the King by signs that it was unhappy there and wanted to go back to the sea. The King, impressed by the creature's religious appearence, did as the Monk-Fish asked and it was returned at once to the beach, where it joyfully dived back into the waves. Apart from the fact that it was supposed to create occasional storms, the Monk-Fish was said to be a harmless creature.

Having found the Monk-Fish, the storytellers of the Middle Ages took only a very short time to find a Bishop-

Fish. This fish was very much like the Monk-Fish except that it wore on its head what seemed to be a Bishop's hat or mitre. Although Bishop-Fish were seen much less frequently than Monk-Fish, one of them is said to have come ashore in Norway in 1526 and lived on land for six days!

The Boneless Bird of Paradise

In 1522 a ship, part of Magellan's around-the-world expedition and now its sole survivor, brought into Seville harbour a rich cargo of spices and also the skins of some fabulously feathered birds. These feathers were the most beautiful men had ever seen. they were long and silky and glowed and shimmered with yellows, oranges and greens. The birds themselves were as light as swansdown and seemed to have no bones, flesh or feet. The beauty of these strange birds excited everyone's interest, particularly the Spanish naturalists who examined them. One said that the birds must live on dew and the nectar of spice trees and that they must certainly be immortal. Another said that because of their lack of feet they were doomed to spend their whole life on the wing, never able to rest for a moment. Others said that they probably did rest by hanging from the trees by their long tail feathers. They all agreed that the birds were completely weightless and feetless and probably came from the Moluccas. Some said, however, that this was untrue and that they could only have come from Paradise, where their corpses fell to earth when they died.

From then on the legend grew and grew and the Bird of Paradise became a bird of God whose special duty it was to protect the warrior in battle. From time to time unpopular naturalists suggested that the birds not only had bones and feet which had been removed but were merely brightly-coloured members of the crow family. No one, of course, believed this, particularly the Dutch and Portuguese ship-owners whose crews were bringing back Birds of Paradise by the dozen. Ladies were buying them at very high prices to make into hats.

This strong belief in the boneless Bird of Paradise continued without faltering for three hundred years, although, in fact, several people knew or had guessed the truth. The

Bird of Paradise

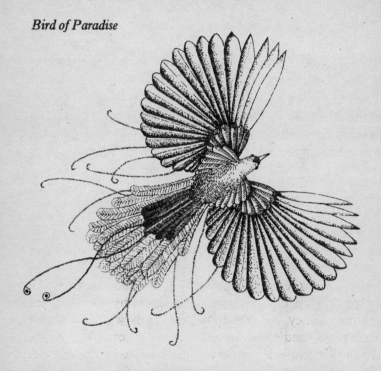

mystery wasn't completely solved until the nineteenth century when René Lesson, a member of the crew of a French ship searching for a lost explorer, spent thirteen days in New Guinea. There he saw many living Birds of Paradise and was fascinated by their beauty. When he returned to France he published a book describing his visit to New Guinea and told of the Birds of Paradise he had seen there.

He also told how he had seen the natives prepare them for the market by removing the bones and certain parts of their skin. They stretched the carcass on a frame and rubbed wood ash into it to harden and preserve it while the framework held the bird in shape. When it was finished it was the light, airy, beautiful creature that was known all over Europe -- so at last this particular legend was shattered.

The Bunyip

The Bunyip is a sort of Australian bogey that was all the rage in the middle of the nineteenth century. The word 'bunyip' is derived from the Aboriginal language, and is thought to mean something like 'devil' or 'spirit'. To the white people in Australia it has come to mean any mysterious animal or

Bunyip

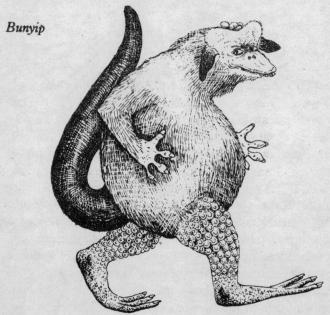

indeed anything at all that is difficult to explain. Reports on the Bunyip are many and various but a surprisingly large number of people claim to have seen it in the flesh – if indeed it has flesh.

Some observers say that it is a species of giant eel that normally eats fish but is not averse to an occasional change in diet when a succulent human comes along. A group of witnesses who saw a Bunyip in Port Fairy, Victoria, said that it was brown with a long, shaggy mane and a head like a kangaroo. They swore that it had strange, hypnotic powers that could transport its victims over water. Other people who have sighted a female Bunyip claim that she is especially dangerous if you threaten her offspring. In revenge, she can make the surface of the water rise, causing serious flooding. If this water should creep over the soles of your shoes it would turn you into a swan. A female Bunyip is to be avoided at all costs.

The Carbuncle

In South America in the sixteenth century the name Carbuncle, meaning ruby or garnet, was given to a very mysterious creature by the Spanish conquerors. It was mysterious because no one seemed to have seen it for long enough to know its shape or size or whether it had fur or feathers. One man, who claimed to have seen it in Paraguay, described it as a smallish animal with a shining mirror on its head like a glowing coal. Another man who saw it claimed that this mirror of light shining out of the darkness was similar to the precious stone dragons were thought to have hidden in their brain! Possession of the Carbuncle jewel brought good fortune and many people searched for it. One man, Barco Centenava, was said to have spent many unhappy years hunting the rivers and jungles of Paraguay for this sly creature. As far as we know he never found it, and there has been no recent news of this beast and its precious gem.

The Catoblepas

In Ethiopia there is said to be a wild beast called the Catoblepas. It moves very sluggishly and has a remarkably heavy head, which the animal finds almost impossible to carry. Fortunately it is unable to lift its head high enough to look at anyone. This is a good thing, as all who look into its eyes are said to fall dead on the spot. The story goes that the poor animal has such problems seeing what it is doing that it once ate its front legs by mistake!

The Centaur

One of the best-known examples of a combined human and animal creature (such as the Lamia and Minotaur, described later in this book) is the Centaur. In early Greek mythology, Centaurs were the top halves of human beings merged with the body and legs of a horse. They were said to live in the mountains of Arcadia and Thessaly. The probable explanation for this surprising creature is that the Greeks of early times, unfamiliar with horseriding, imagined the horsemen of the north to be part of their horses and thought that man and beast were one complete creature.

In mythology the Centaur is highly respected as a noble being. The most famous Centaur was Chiron, renowned for his knowledge of music, medicine and archery. He is said to have taught man how to use various plants and medicinal herbs and passed on his great knowledge to the famous heroes of his age. In spite of his understanding of medicine, however, he was gravely wounded when a poisoned arrow fired by Hercules accidentally pierced his knee. As he was immortal and unable to die, he suffered severe agony until Zeus, the King of the gods, took pity on him and placed him among the stars. To the Greeks he was represented by the constellation Sagittarius, the Archer, the ninth star of the zodiac.

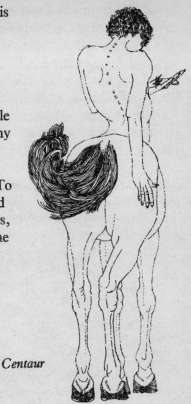

Centaur

Cerberus

In Greek mythology, the entrance to Hades (the Underworld and home of the dead), was guarded by a most ferocious watch-dog, Cerberus, which was said to be a really fearsome sight. Early writers credit him with fifty heads but eventually the number was whittled down to a mere three. He also had six eyes, three mouths, three throats and a triple bark!

Cerberus was the beloved offspring of the serpent-woman Echidna and Typhon, the Greek god of evil, who was so tall that his head actually touched the sky. Cerberus wagged his tail, which was a serpent, to greet all new arrivals to Hades, but tore them to pieces if they attempted to leave. A later legend even has him biting new guests. Relatives of the dead then began to put a piece of honey-cake in the coffin to soothe Cerberus when their dead relatives arrived at the gates of Hades!

Cerberus

The twelfth of Hercules' tasks for King Eurystheus was to capture this three-headed dog and bring him back from Hades. Hercules passed into that gloomy land and asked permission of the King and Queen to borrow Cerberus for a time. They agreed that he could do so, provided he used only his bare hands to capture him. Hercules seized the dog by two of its necks and, holding it in a grip of iron, carried it up to the world above. The hideous hound snapped and snarled but was unable to escape Hercules' strong arms. Later, the dog was returned to its master.

The Chimera

The Chimera was a Greek monster made up of three different animals and was thought to be the sister of Cerberus, the Guardian of Hades. Sometimes it had a lion's front end and a dragon's rear with a she-goat's head sandwiched in between. Sometimes the monster is described as having all the three animal heads at the front, sometimes with a head at each end and one growing from the middle of its back! Whichever Chimera you prefer, it is still a very fierce-looking animal, and is said to have terrorized the people of Lycia, in Asia Minor, where it lived in the mountains.

As far as we know there was only ever one Chimera, a fire-spitting female that devastated the district of Lycia and Caria as well. She was another offspring of Typhon, a hideous monster with a hundred heads, and Echidna, who was a fearful creature, half-woman and half-serpent.

Iobates, King of Lycia, had for many years offered a large reward to whoever could slay this vile beast, and although many a gallant hero had died in the attempt some had returned to tell everyone how impossible the task appeared to be. One day, a youth named Bellerophon appeared at the Court bringing letters with him from Iobates' own son-in-law. The letters gave glowing accounts of Bellerophon's bravery but hinted that, for some evil reason of his own, the writer would be very pleased not to see Bellerophon again. The King decided that the best thing to do would be to send Bellerophon off to tackle the Chimera – either way, one of them would die; if it was the Chimera he would be delighted, if it was Bellerophon then at least his son-in-law would be pleased.

Bellerophon was quite happy to embark on this adventure, but had the good sense to consult a wise fortune-teller before leaving. He was told that he would have little chance of success unless he could get the help of Pegasus, the winged horse that belonged to the goddess Minerva. He was also told to use only lead for his weapons. Although doubtful that such a soft metal could dent the hide of such an awesome creature, Bellerophon did as he was told and took with him a lead-tipped spear.

Bellerophon spent the night in Minerva's temple sleeping and praying, and in the morning he awoke to find that he was holding the golden bridle of the winged horse. As he left the temple he found Pegasus outside, drinking at a well, and had no difficulty in mounting him. He then flew off to find the dreadful Chimera. His task was much easier than he had expected. The Chimera, with its three different parts, was surprisingly slow and clumsy, but Pegasus was quite the opposite. He swooped time and time again, bearing Bellerophon on his back.

On his first attempt Bellerophon's spear rang against the monster's bony side and the tip buckled. Bellerophon went in bravely for a second attempt, knowing that the spear was going to be of little use to him. Suddenly, however, Pegasus made a clever turn in the air and the lead tip of the spear fell into one of the monster's fiery mouths. The searing heat of the Chimera's tongue melted the lump of lead and it trickled, hissing and boiling, down the monster's throat. She died instantly, presumably from lead poisoning!

This was the last of the Chimera, for she was too amazing and unlikely a creature to have been seriously believed in for very long. Her name still lingers in today's language, however, and the word *chimera* is taken to mean a vain or foolish fancy.

Cnoc Na Cnoimh or the Worm of the Hill

In the valley of Cassley in Sutherland, Scotland, there is a strange tale of a fierce and gigantic female worm that laid waste the normally fertile valley and caused the people of the valley to flee from their homes. Almost eight hundred years ago this huge worm made her hole in the side of the valley. Like most worms she could move only slowly, but unfortunately she had very poisonous breath that poured out of her

25

hole like smoke from a volcano, destroying all living things for miles around.

The valley soon became a sad and desolate place. Sometimes the worm would leave her lair and crawl around the summit of the hill, winding her length round and round like a corkscrew and seeming to enjoy the scene of destruction around her.

The King of Scotland offered a reward for anyone brave enough to slay the monster. Many knights came forward but none was successful. At last a rough farmer, Hector Gunn, decided to try, and he made his way to the worm's hill, 'Cnoc na Cnoimh', around which the worm was coiled, sunning herself. He drew his broadsword and galloped forward, meaning to lop off the monster's head. He soon, however, began to feel the effects of the monster's breath, and retreated feeling faint and weak. But Hector Gunn was not a man to be beaten by a worm! He went out to the moors and cut out a large piece of peat, which he pressed on the end of a very long stick. He then dipped the strange weapon in a fire, and at once galloped off to Cnoc na Cnoimh. As Hector drew near, the worm opened her great mouth to pour out her venomous breath and the farmer thrust the smouldering peat towards her. The smoke was so intense and foul-smelling that the monster almost suffocated. In agony she coiled tighter and tighter around the hill.

Hector rode nearer and nearer till he drew level with the writhing thing and with one quick movement thrust the smouldering peat down the creature's throat. He held it there until the monster died. The King of Scotland rewarded him with land and money and the people of the valley were delighted. The deep spiral grooves around Cnoc na Cnoimh made by the worm in her death throes are still there for everyone to see.

The Cyclops

The word *cyclops* means 'round-eyed one', and in Greek legend the Cyclops were a race of giants with one eye placed in the middle of their foreheads. These monsters lived on their own island as shepherds. They were shaggy, hairy creatures who lived in caves and fed themselves on mutton. Odysseus, a famous Greek warrior returning from the Trojan War, found his ship blown off course by a gale. The winds blew them on to the island of the Cyclops and, little realizing their danger, Odysseus and his crew explored the island and found a cave well stocked with food. This particular cave belonged to the one-eyed giant Polyphemus, the biggest and fiercest Cyclops of all. When the giant returned home he drove his sheep into the cave and closed the entrance with an enormous boulder. Odysseus made himself known to the monster and pleaded with him for food and shelter, telling him of the ten years they had spent fighting in the Trojan War. The giant did not answer. He just picked up two of Odysseus's crew, hurled them at the wall of the cave, and then snatched them up and ate them. He washed down his meal with a bowl of milk and lay down to sleep. Odysseus and the rest of the crew were horrified! They were hopelessly trapped and dared not attempt to kill Polyphemus, for they could not hope to move the boulder by themselves. The next morning Polyphemus woke up and made his breakfast of two more of Odysseus's companions before leaving the cave with his sheep.

While he was away, Odysseus and his friends sharpened the end of the wooden pole which the giant used as a staff and hardened it in the fire. They then hid it under a pile of straw. When Polyphemus returned in the evening he once again made a meal of two men, drank a bowl of wine and lay down to sleep. He was soon snoring loudly and Odysseus and his remaining men crept forward with the sharpened pole and twisted it into the giant's only eye. Polyphemus leapt up, groaning and raging. He stumbled blindly about the cave but could do nothing to ease the pain. The next morning the Cyclops left the cave again with his sheep but, as he could no longer see, Odysseus and his men were able to hang under the bellies of the sheep as they passed through the mouth of the cave into the fields. Polyphemus felt the backs and sides of the sheep in case the Greeks were riding on their backs, but his groping fingers did not find them hidden underneath.

Cyclops

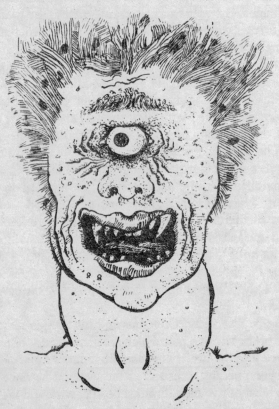

The men escaped to their boat, taking as many sheep as possible with them for food. They were chased by the Cyclops, who almost wrecked their boat by throwing mighty boulders into the sea, but they managed to escape and continued on their journey.

Dinosaurs

Of all the monsters, real or mythical, perhaps most extraordinary are a group of extinct reptiles that lived on our planet over one hundred million years ago. Today we call them Dinosaurs. The fossilized remains and footprints of Dinosaurs found in rocks show that there were, in fact, more than five thousand kinds, from tiny to gigantic. The word *dinosaur* means 'terror lizard' but, in spite of their name, the largest of them excite more interest today than any other creatures of the past. Museum visitors flock to the Dinosaur exhibits to gaze at their huge, outlandish shapes and wonder what life must have been like when these 'terror lizards' roamed the earth. Dinosaurs are also portrayed in comics, cartoons and stories, usually in places where they have no business to be, and often keeping company with cavemen. Some people have also suggested that the great Sea Serpents and the Loch Ness Monster are types of Dinosaur! As far as we know, however, Dinosaurs became extinct many millions of years before man even came on the scene. The time they did spend on earth, however, is by no means negligible - they completely dominated the land for about a hundred million years, which is a long time by anybody's reckoning!

During that long period many strange forms of reptiles developed. The great Dinosaurs of the Jurassic period were the largest animals that have ever lived. Some became so large and heavy that they could move only very slowly on four legs. Others grew just as big but taught themselves to walk upright on their back legs. As a result of this their back legs grew thick and strong whilst their front legs got shorter and weaker until they could hardly be used at all. They used their long muscular tails to help themselves to balance, in the same way as a kangaroo does. To protect themselves against their enemies some Dinosaurs were covered in thick, scaly skin like armour-plating, which certainly made them look frightening. Other Dinosaurs were more gentle, bird-like creatures.

Probably the best-known Dinosaur is the *Brontosaurus* or 'Thunder Lizard'. It was about 20 metres (70 feet) long and weighed 41 tonnes (40 tons) – which is more than ten

Brontosaurus

elephants! In spite of its large and ferocious appearance it lived entirely on plants and had a very small brain weighing only about half a kilogram (1 pound). Its large body and small brain must have made it a very stupid, slow-moving creature. It stood on four legs, and had a long tail and a long neck with a very small head on the end of it. As it had such a tiny mouth and such a large stomach to fill, it spent its entire life eating and dozing. It could usually be seen wading about in shallow lakes and rivers eating plants. Its nostrils and eyes were on top of its head so that it could still breathe and see when almost entirely covered by water. Such a sluggish, slow-moving animal had no way of defending itself from the fierce flesh-eating land Dinosaurs so it probably kept in the water to avoid them and, of course, to take some of the weight off its legs!

Its cousin was the *Diplodocus*, which was even longer than the Brontosaurus but with a long tail shaped like a whip. It was much lighter than the Brontosaurus. Together with the *Brachiosaurus*, another sort of gigantic reptile, it was harmless and gentle and lived completely on plants from the sea bed. These placid creatures might have been alive for even longer than a hundred million years had it not been for their deadly enemies, the savage, carnivorous land Dinosaurs. One of these, the *Allosaurus*, was about 9 metres (35 feet) long and walked upright. It stalked and killed animals many times larger than itself and seemed to be completely fearless. The most terrible of all Dinosaurs, however, was the *Tyrannosaurus Rex* (meaning 'King of the Tyrants'). This monster was 15 metres (50 feet) long and 7½ metres (25 feet) high with an impressive row of teeth, each about 15 centimetres (6 inches) long, set in enormous vice-like jaws. Like the Allosaurus it walked on its powerful, sharply clawed hind legs and used its front limbs as hands to catch hold of its prey and tear it apart. Its head and brain were larger than those of other Dinosaurs and it could run and jump at great speed. It spent its entire day killing, eating and sleeping and no other

living creature was safe from it! Needless to say, this species managed to outlive many of the other Dinosaurs.

One of its favourite meals was the *Trachodon*. This was an enormous, odd-looking creature with a duck's bill. It looked rather like a web-footed kangaroo. The oddest thing about these duck-billed Dinosaurs was the amazing number of teeth they had. The trachodon had no teeth in the front of its bill but two rows of five hundred on each side of it, making two thousand altogether! One of the very few times it came on to dry land was to lay its eggs and then, of course, it had to keep its eye open for a stalking Tyrannosaurus Rex! At one time there were also Dinosaurs with horns, like the *Triceratops*. This had three evil-looking horns and a tough shield of hide over its neck to protect it from its enemies. It was built like a tank and even its eyes were protected by a piece of overhanging bone. In spite of being a vegetarian it was still a fierce fighter and was sometimes known to send off even the Tyrannosaurus Rex with its tail between its legs.

In order to understand the Dinosaurs and their history they should be looked at in their own environment and against a background of the long history of the earth. There are many interesting Dinosaur skeletons and other information in the Natural History Museum in London.

Triceratops

Dragons

Of all the fabulous, frightening beasts in the world, the Dragon is the King. His supreme power and majesty were worshipped at some time or another by almost every race in the world. He was already extremely old when the very first myths were written down. His character varies from East to West; in the East, he represents the power of nature, particularly when connected with water. Sometimes he can be mischievous, but on the whole he is thought of as a kindly beast. The Western Dragon, on the other hand is utterly evil.

Dragons of the West

For all his wickedness the Dragon was still looked on as a symbol of strength and power. The Dragon was adopted as a warlike emblem very early on and Vikings used to paint rampant Dragons on their shields and carve Dragons' heads on the prows of their ships. In England, in the days before the Norman Conquest, the Dragon was the most popular symbol in times of war and the name 'Pendragon' was a title given to a knight who had killed a chief in battle or done some other

Western Dragon

heroic deed. In the tales of King Arthur and the Knights of the Round Table, Arthur's father was given the title Uther Pendragon and was allowed to carry a shining gold Dragon on his personal flag. In the sixteenth century a new musket was invented which spurted fire when it was set off at the enemy. It was immediately likened to Dragons' breath and the muzzles were decorated with Dragons breathing fire and smoke. The mounted soldiers who carried the muskets were called dragoons, a name which is still used today.

The head of a Western Dragon

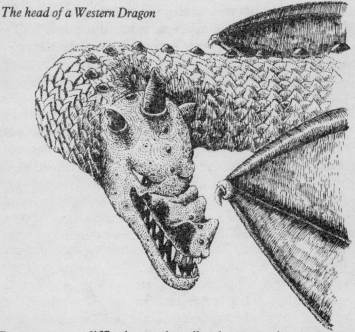

Dragons are difficult to describe because they vary so much from time to time and place to place, but the Western Dragon is usually a heavy-looking Serpent with wings and claws. It can be any colour, even black, as long as it shines brilliantly and can belch forth fire and smoke. It is always huge, with a hideous scaly body and broad wings set vertically across it (not like a bird's wings, which are horizontal).

It often spreads its wings, but for some reason rarely uses them for flying. Its fiery breath has been known to destroy entire cities. It makes its home in deserted areas of scrublands, caves, mountains and other remote places. At all times it is the enemy of man, a terrifying, harmful creature of darkness.

All Western Dragons are very rich, but unlike the dragons of the East they are extremely miserly and hide their riches away. They have mountainous piles of gold and jewels which they hide under the earth or at the bottom of very deep rivers where no man can reach them, and as they are so mean they fight to the death any man who would try to steal it. The famous Scandinavian hero Beowulf fought a battle with a Dragon who had hidden its gold near Beowulf's castle. Although Beowulf died as a result of his wounds he lived long enough to see the incredible hoard of gold and jewels found in the Dragon's lair. One of Beowulf's knights killed the dragon, and Beowulf and the Dragon's gold were buried together on a nearby headland which was rechristened 'Beowulf' so that all the ships that passed by would never forget his name.

ST GEORGE'S DRAGON

The real story of St George's Dragon is so far in the past now that no one is really sure exactly which George was concerned, where the battle took place and if in fact a Dragon was killed at all. It seems as if it is just another symbolic story of the triumph of good over evil. The following is one of the most popular versions, which has been celebrated in England since 1222, when it was decreed that a national festival should be held every year on 23 April in honour of the saint.

George was not English but an Eastern saint, supposed to have slain a Dragon in his youth, whose fame had been carried to England by the early Crusaders. He was born in

36

Asia Minor and when he was a young man, in the days before Christianity was widespread, he travelled to the town of Silene near Libya to become a Christian.

In a lake outside Silene there lived an evil Dragon which climbed over the city walls every night killing people with its poisonous breath and devouring their bodies. Most people had been unable to go to bed for months, afraid of being eaten in their sleep. The King had sent in many armies to attack the Dragon but none had been successful. Finally the people of the city had the idea of feeding the Dragon themselves to prevent it from coming into the city. For a time the Dragon was happy to eat two sheep a day, but when they ran out of sheep the Dragon once more began clambering over the walls every night. As there were no more animals to be found the people decided to give the Dragon one human being every day, the poor unfortunate being chosen by drawing lots. Whilst one person became the Dragon's dinner, at least the rest could get a decent night's sleep!

Finally the day came when the lot fell upon the King's daughter, Princess Saba. She put on her best clothes and, saying goodbye to her father, made her way to the edge of the city. She was standing there, waiting and weeping, when she was approached by George. He was horrified when the princess told him she was waiting for the Dragon to come from the lake and eat her up.

'Don't be afraid,' he said. 'In the name of Christ I will slay this Dragon.'

The lake then began to swirl and bubble as the Dragon lurched to the surface. George jumped on his horse and arrived at the lake just as the Dragon was poking its head through the water. Closing his helmet to prevent the Dragon's poisonous breath reaching him, he said a prayer, made a sign of the Cross and then plunged his lance into the writhing beast. The Dragon lashed its tail around in a frenzy and George told the princess to take off her jewelled belt and to tie up the Dragon with it whilst he held it down with his

37

lance. The terrified princess did so and the Dragon straight-away became quiet and gentle.

The princess climbed up on George's horse and together they rode back to town, followed by the obedient Dragon. When the people saw the strange threesome they rushed back home in terror, so George struck the head off the Dragon so it would never frighten anyone again. He then baptized everyone in the name of the new religion, Christianity.

THE BEN VAIR DRAGON

Ben Vair in Scotland, where tourists to Glencoe in Argyll are landed, takes its name from the Dragon that used to live in a great hollow in the face of the mountain known as Corrie Lia. This Dragon, of traditional appearance apparently, used to peer over the path that wound around the foot of the mountain and would leap down and tear to pieces anyone it caught passing by.

The Dragon, a female, was so terrifying that no one dared to approach her until 'Charles the Skipper' came to Ben Vair. He anchored his boat some way from the shore and built a bridge of empty wooden barrels between the boat and the shore. He lashed them together with ropes and struck iron spikes into them until they looked like floating porcupines. When the bridge was finished he lit a fire on board his boat and began to roast some large pieces of meat.

The delicious smell of roasting meat drifted across the water and into the lair of the Corrie Lia Dragon. Her great nostrils sniffed the air rapturously and she leapt from the cave with a mighty bound. Taking the spiked bridge at a headlong run, she was soon slowed down by the spikes! The needle-sharp points pierced her scales and she was fatally wounded. Charles the Skipper had left a gap between the last barrel and his boat, but the Dragon had not enough strength to try to leap it, and she died at the end of the bridge. There is a rock upon which Ben Vair House now stands, called Leac-na-Beithreach, or Dragon Rock.

WELSH DRAGONS

On St David's Day patriotic Welshmen fly the flag of *Y Ddraig Goch* – a red Dragon with extended wings on two horizontal bars of white and green. When Great Britain and Ireland were united in 1284, a red Dragon on a green mount was made the official badge of Wales and the Prince of Wales had the red Dragon added to his coat of arms. No one knows for sure how long the red Dragon has been so strongly connected with Wales or how it came about, but the following explanation is very popular.

In the fifth century, after the Romans had come to Britain, King Vortigern fled with his twelve wise men to the foot of Mt Snowdon in Wales, which was very wild in those days. He decided to settle there and ordered a great fortress to be built for him at a place called Dinas Emrys. The workmen worked hard every day on the foundations of the building and prepared piles of hewn stones and shaped timbers, but every night the ground swallowed them up again. This happened so regularly that the workmen were convinced that a wicked spell had been put on them. The King consulted his wise men about the strange behaviour of the foundations and they told him that the only way to break the spell was to find a fatherless boy and sprinkle his blood on the ground where the fortress was to be built. The King's men set out to look for such a child, and in Carmarthen they found a seven-year-old boy called Merlin.

Before the King had a chance to kill the boy, however, Merlin told him just what was really happening under the foundations. The child, who had a gift for seeing into the future, explained that underneath the fortress was a deep pool inhabited by two Dragons, one red and one white. Every night they fought so fiercely that they cracked the foundation walls. On the King's orders the workmen dug until they found the pool and the two sleeping Dragons, which soon awoke and began fighting again. Merlin told the King that the two Dragons really represented the two British nations; the red one was Celtic and the white one was Saxon. He foretold that for many, many years there would be wars and chaos while the two nations fought but that one day the red Dragon would become the emblem of Wales. The site of the fortress would move to South Wales, where it would soon be successfully completed. King Vortigern spared Merlin's life and he grew up to be Merlin the magician, known throughout Europe for his prophecies.

Welsh Dragons, like Dragons the world over, were supposed to be very rich. Some of them even wore precious stones or had gold rings in their tails. Others demanded gifts of small children for their breakfast and quite often devoured whole flocks of sheep at a sitting. Welsh Dragons usually lived at the bottom of lakes or guarded holy places like wells or springs. There are a great many Welsh Dragon legends, and even St George was said to have come to Wales and slain at least one of them. In West Wales a monstrous Dragon with poisonous breath destroyed many acres of countryside until St Samson threw him into the sea. A flying Dragon was said to have lived in the Vale of Neath, where it guarded its hoard of treasure in a lonely gorge. These flying Dragons were particularly colourful and could often be seen flying about at midnight moving their treasures from one hiding-place to another.

The town of Denbigh was said to have received its name after a nobleman had slain the local Dragon. When he carried the Dragon's head through the town the people greeted him, shouting '*Dim bych, Dim bych*' – which means 'no more Dragons'. Denbigh still keeps the name. Dragons are still to be found in modern Wales, on churches, heraldic shields, shops and sometimes even on weather vanes. On public buildings the Dragon flag flies proud and fierce. *Y Ddraig Goch Ddyry Chchwyn* – the Red Dragon takes the lead.

Dragons of the East

The great Chinese dictionary *Pan Tsao Kang Mu*, written about AD 1600, has a lot to say about Dragons. The Dragon, it tells us, is the largest of scaled creatures. Its head is like a camel's, its ears like a bull's, its neck like a snake's, its belly like a frog's, its scales like a carp's, its claws like and eagle's and its paw like a tiger's. It has eighty-one scales, nine rows by nine (numbers that are said to be lucky) and its voice is like the beating of a gong. It has whiskers around its mouth, a pearl under its chin and on top of its head is the *poh shan* which looks like a wooden ruler, somehow used by the Dragon to soar up to the skies.

The Dragons of the East are too numerous to count, for they are everywhere where there is water. They populate the deepest seas and the shallowest rivers down to the tiniest drop of rain, and they are completely in charge of weather conditions. A flash of lightning is the Dragon flashing his eyes, the wind is his breath and storms at sea are caused by the tearing of his claws. The pearl which the Dragon carries under his chin is said to be a symbol of the sun and the source of all his power. Without the pearl he would be helpless.

During important celebrations in China a paper Dragon is always carried through the streets in a procession. A man must run before it carrying a large red or white ball, representing the magic pearl which the Dragon is always vainly trying to catch. According to its own wishes the Dragon can become visible or invisible. In springtime it goes up into the skies and in autumn it descends into the depths of the sea.

There are several different kinds of Dragon responsible for the running of the world. The *Celestial Dragon* carries on his back the palaces of the gods that might otherwise fall on to the earth's cities and destroy them. The *Divine Dragon* makes the winds and rain, the *Terrestrial Dragon* looks after streams and rivers and decides which way they should flow, and the *Subterranean Dragon* guards the treasures that are forbidden to man. The Chinese people still believe that the Dragons look after them very well, and usually everything runs smoothly. When there is a lack of water or a flood – and there have been many dreadful floods in China – the Chinese people are worried, for they know that something must have caused the Dragon-kings to be angry.

If there is a flood they throw jewels and prayers written on paper into the torrent, hoping to make their peace with the Dragon. If it is a drought they are worried about, then another paper Dragon is made and carried through the streets. It calls at every house in the village and everyone who answers the door sprinkles it with water. A watercarrier also runs beside the Dragon, sprinkling the ground and shouting, 'Here comes the Rain!'

As Dragons are so powerful it can be disastrous to offend them, so if one intends to keep on the right side of them there are a few things to remember. The most important one is their passion for eating swallows. The Dragons are so keen on this particular food themselves that they become very fierce if they find out that a man has also eaten some. Under no circumstances must a man who has ever eaten swallows cross the water, because any Dragon that happens to be living there will rise up and devour him in a flash!

The Sea-Dragon kings, yet another kind of ruler, live in lavish underwater palaces and feed on opals and pearls. There are five of these kings: the chief, who lives in the middle, and four others who live at the four points of the compass. Each Dragon is 5 or 6 kilometres (3 or 4 miles) long, and if they so much as turn over in the night they can cause whole mountains to fall into the sea. They also have whiskery snouts, but their scales are yellow. They have shaggy legs and tails and wild flaming eyes. Their mouths constantly hang open and show their long tongues and sharp teeth, and when they breathe heavily they can cook a whole shoal of passing fish. If these Sea-Dragons come up to the surface of the sea they cause whirlpools, typhoons and whirlwinds. When they fly they cause the kind of hurricane that tears off the roofs of entire cities and causes terrible flood damage.

No one knows why Dragons have these violent bursts of temper that create so much havoc for, in spite of their reputation for being fatherly and kind, they do seem to be moody and unreliable. They are also said to be vain. A story tells us that one great Emperor, the one who built the Great Wall of China, wished to visit one of the most important Sea-Dragons. This Dragon-king agreed to the meeting provided that the Emperor and his men made no attempt to draw a picture of him. He made this strange condition because he was very ugly indeed. He even had the men searched to make sure they were not carrying any drawing-paper or brushes.

During the meeting, however, one man was so hypnotized by the hideousness of the Dragon-king, made worse by the fact that he was wearing a beautiful crown, that he began absent-mindedly drawing a picture of him in the sand with his foot. When the Dragon noticed what he was doing he leapt to his feet in a violent rage and started a storm that was to last for a week. The Emperor himself managed to swim ashore but the rest of the men who went with him were drowned, and once more the homes of many innocent people were destroyed. However, the Chinese people still love the Dragon and, unlike the people of the Western world, would be delighted to meet one any day of the week!

TIAMAT – THE DRAGON OF BABYLONIA
One of the earliest legendary Dragons was Tiamat of Babylonia. She was supposed to be the beautiful, female Dragon of Confusion. She lived in the sea in the days before human life began, when the earth was nothing but sea and sky.

Tiamat had the future of the world written on slabs of stone and she held on to them firmly, because she knew that whoever held them had control of the world. The gods of Babylonia, who came to life some time after Tiamat, lived in the sky and wanted to make the world a more orderly place, but they could do nothing whilst Tiamat had the stone tablets. So they decided to kill her. They were unsuccessful because she had magic powers which destroyed all kinds of weapons – even magic spells could not be worked against her.

At last the gods gave Marduk, the supreme god, all their special powers and sent him forth to do battle with the Dragon. He took bows and arrows, a flash of lightning and an enormous net filled with wind. He found Tiamat sitting on a large rock in the middle of the ocean. When the Dragon saw Marduk coming towards her she began to laugh at him, but Marduk kept on coming. This annoyed Tiamat and she opened her mouth in a mighty rage. Marduk threw the net over her and let the winds loose. They held her mouth open while Marduk sent first the lightning, followed by the arrow, down her throat. The arrow pierced her heart and she died immediately.

Once Tiamat was dead, Marduk cut her body into two pieces; one became the earth and the other the heavens. This was the Babylonians' theory of the way the world was created. The story of Marduk and Tiamat became the symbol of good being victorious over evil.

Fox Spirits

The Chinese fox differs very little in appearance from foxes found anywhere else in the world but appearances, of course, can be deceptive! Oriental foxes are said to have a life-span of up to a thousand years, and have a different magic power for each part of their body. This strange Fox Spirit is also considered to be a very bad omen, probably because he can start a fire merely by banging his tail upon the ground. He can see into the future and change into many forms, but usually chooses old men or young women. He makes his home near a graveyard and gets his greatest pleasure from playing nasty pranks on people and causing them hurt and discomfort. There are many thousands of stories telling of his exploits.

The Japanese people have a similar Fox Spirit with the same magical powers as the Chinese fox. Sometimes the Japanese Fox Spirit can be identified by a strange spurt of flame that can be seen flickering over his head, usually only for a few seconds. There are, however, other ways of identifying the crafty Fox Spirit. If you should catch a human being behaving in a supicious manner you can always stand him in front of a pool of water. If he really is a Fox Spirit, you will see the reflection of a fox in the water, and once caught in this way he will run off as quickly as he can. Another method is to produce a dog, for the sight of a dog, which he greatly fears, will cause him to resume his true form at once.

Unfortunately, this applies only to foxes younger than a thousand years old. If you should be unfortunate enough to come up against one older than that there is only one thing left for you to do. Find a tree exactly the same age as the fox,

Fox Spirit

cut it down, light a fire with it and let the light shine on the fox. This apparently never fails! If a Fox Spirit should live longer than a thousand years he usually turns white or golden and sprouts nine tails. His magic powers get stronger and he goes up to heaven, where it is no longer necessary to play tricks on humans. These Fox Spirits, both Chinese and Japanese, are said to have a magic pearl which gives them most of their power; sometimes it is carried in the mouth and sometimes in one of the fox's nine tails.

In the twelfth century the Emperor of Japan had a woman friend called Tomamo No Mae, or the Jewel Maiden, who, besides being the most beautiful woman in the land, had also a happy and charming personality. She was the Emperor's favourite friend and constant companion. One evening the Emperor held a very lavish banquet in his summer palace. Suddenly, in the middle of the meal, a clap of thunder was heard outside and all the lights went out. A strange cold wind blew through the palace and made the people shiver! Then the Emperor called out for a light. Suddenly, a luminous yellow flame spurted out of the head of the Jewel Maiden, filling the whole palace with light.

From that day onwards the Emperor's health began to suffer; he became gradually weaker and finally took to his bed without any of his doctors having an idea what was wrong with him. Finally a magician was called in to give his opinion and he at once declared that the illness must have been caused by the Jewel Maiden who, because of her behaviour at the banquet, must be a Fox Spirit. The word 'fox' brought a wild scream from somewhere in the palace, and a large white fox was seen to run through the front door crying 'Ko-Ko', which is the fox's call. The Emperor's guards chased after the fox and killed it. The spirit of the fox lived on, however, in a large stone nearby. For over a hundred years this stone was known as the Death Stone, as no bird would land on it and no man or animal could stray near it without being overcome by its poisonous fumes.

Dr Frankenstein's Monster

Somewhere in a creepy East European country (no one quite knows where) a Dr Henry Frankenstein works at home, in Castle Frankenstein, on a fascinating hobby. He enjoys building men with odd human bits and pieces in the strange hope that one day he will get all the right bits together at the right time and, with the help of some electricity, bring them to life in the form of a human person. The day comes when all the right pieces are assembled, including the brain of an executed murderer brought along by Frankenstein's deformed assistant, Hugo, and the scientist is all ready to put life into the thing he has created. During a violent electrical storm the artificial man is slowly lifted up to an opening in the roof, where its body is struck time and time again by bolts of lightning. Gradually the body begins to stir and eventually comes to life. Unfortunately, however, Dr Frankenstein soon discovers that the artificial man has not turned out as he planned and that instead of building a man he has created a fearsome monster.

The story of Frankenstein's Monster, originally written in the early nineteenth century by Mary Shelley, the wife of the English poet Percy Shelley, was eventually turned into one of the most famous horror films of all time. It was first made in 1931, but the Monster created on film lives on to frighten us even today. The actor who played the part of the Monster, Boris Karloff, was worked on by make-up men for hours every day, using many pounds of make-up, to turn his ordinary face into that of a sub-human monster. When he was finished his head was flat-topped with sunken eyes and huge bulging eyebrows. Two large metal bolts appeared to be screwed into the sides of his neck so that electricity could flow into his body. There were also livid scars where his hands had been sewn on to his arms. There have been many

47

film monsters since 1931, but none has been more gruesome and difficult to forget than Frankenstein's Monster.

The story of the film tells how Frankenstein keeps the Monster imprisoned in the castle until one day he bursts his chains, kills Hugo and runs into the country, where he meets a little girl who speaks kindly to him. For a moment it seems as if he will become quiet and reasonable, but after a few minutes he throws the child into the water and leaves her to drown. The Monster now keeps on running, pursued by Frankenstein and an angry mob of villagers. Finally the Monster and his creator meet on a mountaintop, where the Monster overpowers Frankenstein and carries him inside a windmill. The windmill is surrounded by the villagers, who set it on fire. Frankenstein struggles to get free and, in the

Frankenstein's Monster

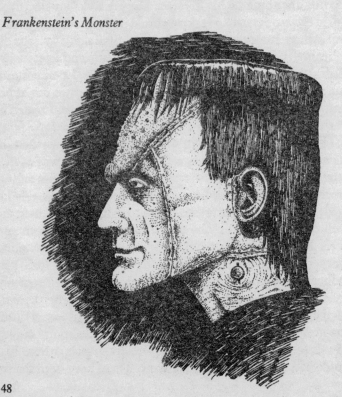

fight that follows, the Monster throws Frankenstein out of the window, breaking his arm. The doctor is very lucky, as it turns out, for it is already too late for the Monster to escape and, as the villagers cheer, the windmill burns down with the Monster inside it.

The film *Frankenstein* was so successful that a sequel, *Bride of Frankenstein*, was filmed four years later. In this film a hideous female figure was created. It turned out to be even more terrifying than the first film and a great success at the box office! Many other sequels followed – both serious and comic.

Ganesha

Ganesha is a well-known figure in the myths and legends of India. He usually appears with a fat, human body equipped with four arms and hands and a head like an elephant's. He has only one tusk instead of two and this is white, with the rest of his body coloured bright red. He usually rides on the back of a once-powerful demon, which he has now tamed and changed into an ordinary rat. Many stories are told about Ganesha and his missing tusk, but the fact that they are all so different seems to show that the real explanation has long since been forgotten. Wherever he came from, Ganesha is still thought of as a kindly god who brings wealth, wisdom and good luck. He is also the god of merchants and almost every shopkeeper has his own little statue of the elephant-man. It is said that even today, if a merchant loses all his money, all the Ganeshas in his office are turned upside down.

Many of the tales about Ganesha's tusk seem to be concerned with his love of sweet food and his reluctance to take any exercise, even though he was said to be strong and brave. In one story he stuffed himself so full of buns that he felt in desperate need of some fresh air and, being unwilling

actually to walk anywhere, he mounted his rat and set off for a late-night ride. As he rode along, however, a snake slithered across his path and the rat reared up and threw Ganesha off his back. He hit the ground with such force that his stomach popped like a balloon and the cakes were scattered everywhere. Not wishing the cakes to be wasted, he picked them all up and pushed them back inside his stomach. Snatching up the snake who had caused all the trouble, he wound it around his waist to keep the cakes from falling out again!

When he had finished he was surprised to hear the sound of loud laughter and, looking up, he saw that the moon and the twenty-seven stars who were his wives were very amused to see Ganesha stuffing his stomach with cakes! Angry at being made to look foolish, Ganesha pulled out one of his tusks and hurled it at the grinning face of the moon, hitting it so hard that its light was completely put out. This now meant dark, moonless nights for the earth's people and made things very easy for robbers and others who do evil things under the cover of darkness. The earth's people complained bitterly to the gods. Ganesha finally allowed the moon to shine on some nights and put a curse on it so that every so often it would waste away to nothing. Today we call this the waning of the moon.

The elephant is the traditional Indian enemy of the evil serpent, so this probably had something to do with the original Ganesha being the protector of mankind.

Garuda

One of the most ancient creatures in any mythology of the world is Garuda. He was the divine bird of India, described as being the bird of life – 'destroyer of all, creator of all'. In the very beginning, before history was written down, man made into a god anything he could not understand. Garuda, apparently, was one of the greatest gods of all. Of all the great birds that looked down on to the earth, like the Phoenix, the Roc and the Senmurv, he was the very first, the father of them all.

In the beginning he must have been a bird, but over the years he gradually developed a human body with an eagle's head, claws and wings. His body shone gold in the sun, his face was white and his wings were red. Garuda was the enemy of all serpents, who were thought to be evil, and he used to eat one daily. Before long there were very few snakes left, so a Buddhist prince offered himself as a sacrifice to the gaint bird, as he felt so sorry for the serpents. Garuda was touched by this, and because of it took up the Buddhist religion of kindness to all living things.

The worship of Garuda, which began in India, spread eastwards and he was soon popular in Cambodia (Kampuchea), Siam (Thailand) and Indo-China. His half-man, half-bird figure can be seen in many places in Asia, usually holding a serpent in either hand. He eventually arrived in Japan, where he became mixed up with the Tengu, a similar man-bird but with a very unpleasant nature (described later in this book).

Grendel – The Monster of the Fens

The epic poem *Beowulf* was written shortly before the year AD 750, most probably in Northumbria. No one has ever discovered who wrote it, but it is one of the oldest and longest complete poems in existence and is said to be the earliest work of Anglo-Saxon genius still surviving. It is particularly interesting because it shows us how the people of that period behaved and thought – particularly about monsters. *Beowulf* is the story of the great Danish hero of the same name and his battle with Grendel, the monster of the fens. Grendel was described as being a mighty, monstrous fiend who patrolled the moors and fens near the stronghold of the Danish King Hrothgar. He was not, however, a happy monster, (monsters rarely are), and was said to have been banished by God at the same time that God punished Cain for killing his brother Abel. Grendel was made even more unhappy by the banqueting hall that the Danes had recently built. It was said to be the greatest and most wonderful banqueting hall ever seen, and its graceful gables towered high over the fenlands. Every day Grendel heard the sound of harp music and the happy voices of the warriors singing and reciting poetry. Their happiness grated on his ears and he felt jealous and peevish.

One night, Grendel decided to go down to the banqueting hall under cover of darkness to have a closer look. Inside he found a band of warriors lying asleep after enjoying themselves at a banquet. He pounced on thirty of them as they slept, gobbled them up, and then returned to his lair. His terrible action caused panic and despair among the Danes, particularly as this first attack seemed to have given Grendel the taste for human flesh. Night after night he roamed the fenlands, pouncing on anyone he happened to find and devouring them. The great hall soon lay derelict and the Danish King and his people were stricken with grief. Yet the monster, a black shadow of death, still prowled the fog-bound moors. This went on for twelve years. No one knew what to do about Grendel. The Danes had offered him anything he desired if only he would leave them alone, but he ignored them. He had been tasting blood for too long; it was

Grendel

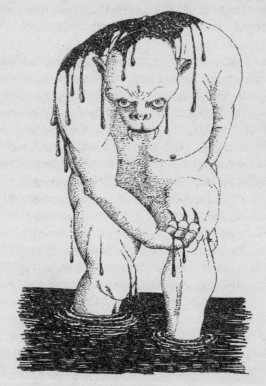

too late to stop now! King Hrothgar held many councils of war, but no one came up with an answer that worked.

One day, when things seemed to be as black as they could be, a ship, armed with fierce-looking warriors, arrived at the beach. The men were from a race of people called the Geats and were led by the brave warrior Beowulf. They had heard of the troubles of King Hrothgar and his people, and had come to offer their services against mighty Grendel. The King was delighted to see Beowulf, whom he recognized as being a distant relative, and gave a banquet for him and his men in the great banqueting hall. After the meal, which was a happy one, Beowulf insisted that he and his men should be left alone in the banqueting hall while the King and his people went to bed. They knew that, as soon as night fell, Grendel would come down from the moors to see what all the excitement was about, and Beowulf was eager to do battle with him.

The monster Grendel strode out of the fog-ridden fens that night looking for excitement. He was amazed to see the great hall ablaze with light and the tables weighed down with the best solid gold plate. He hurried down to the massive door, which was usually fastened with wrought-iron bars, and found it opened to the touch of his talon. An evil fury took hold of him, and he tore down the entire entrance of the building and stepped inside. His hideous eyes glowed like burning coals and he laughed when he saw the rows of sleeping warriors. What a feast he would have tonight! Snatching up the man nearest the door, he crunched him up and swallowed him. The next man he attempted to eat was Beowulf himself, but the hero was too quick for him. Jumping to his feet, he gripped Grendel as tightly as he could and Grendel soon realized that for the first time in his life he had met his match.

The beast tried to break loose and rush back to his lair in the fens, but this time it was too late. They fought together so fiercely that every bench and seat in the place was uprooted, and Grendel began to scream and wail in hideous despair. He seemed to have fallen into the clutches of the strongest man alive. Grendel had an enormous wound in his shoulder and was suffering great pain. Finally, Beowulf allowed him to leave and he returned to his lair in the fens to die.

The banqueting hall was badly wrecked and only the roof was left by the time the battle was over, but the Danish people did not mind. They were pleased to be rid of Grendel at any cost. The King gave Beowulf an embroidered banner of gold, a helmet, a suit of armour and a jewel-studded sword. He also rewarded the men who travelled with him. This is only the first of Beowulf's battles with monsters. Later in the poem he pits his strength against Grendel's mother, and he dies at the end of the poem after a fierce fight with a Dragon, described earlier in this book.

Beowulf has been translated into modern English and makes exciting reading. Only one manuscript still exists (the others were presumably destroyed during the violent wars of the period); this last precious document, after being slightly damaged itself by a house fire in 1731, is now safely stored in the British Museum in London. It was made by scribes about a thousand years ago, two hundred years after the poem was actually composed.

The Griffon (Gryphon, Griffin)

The Griffon is one of the oldest and most popular beasts in heraldry, and even today it appears on many coats of arms. It is half-bird and half-mammal with the wings and head of an eagle, though many times larger, and the rear end, hind legs and tail of a lion. The enormous eagle's head has pointed, upstanding ears like those of a horse. The Griffon was supposed to combine the qualities of the lion, the king of beasts, with those of the eagle, the king of birds. The front claws of

the Griffon were thought by the people of the Middle Ages to be a lucky charm bestowed only on those holy men who were thought likely to be able to cure the Griffon of some serious sickness. The ground-up Griffon's claw was then sold as a cure for almost any sort of illness.

Griffons were said to be amazingly powerful and as strong as a hundred eagles. One claw of this immense monster was the size of two lions and could carry two yoked oxen with ease. According to medieval legends the mighty Griffon built its nest and lined it with a fabulous fortune in gold. It did not lay eggs in its nest like a bird but laid a variety of large gems instead. The beasts were known to the people of India and ancient Greece as the guardians of a great deal of hidden treasure in Scythia, an ancient land somewhere between India and Persia. No one dared to interfere with the Griffon except the Arimaspians, a race of one-eyed Scythian people who loved gold and used it to plait into their long hair. Sometimes they would creep stealthily around the Griffon's nest and try to steal his gold, but the creature's horse-like ears were very sharp and when he found the thieves, he would quickly tear them to pieces with vast claws.

The legend of the Griffon is one of the oldest we know. A tiny model of a golden beast found to be over three thousand years old was discovered in the royal tombs in Crete. It matched identically the Griffon of the Middle Ages, apart from the tail, which was not tufted like the lion's. The only Griffon we see today is on coats of arms, sometimes as a head, but usually rampant. It can be seen in the arms of the City of London, and there is a statue of a Griffon on the pedestal which marks the boundary of the City of London on the site of the old Temple Bar.

The Hai Ho Shang or Sea Bonze

The terror of the South China Seas is the Hai Ho Shang, or Sea Bonze. It is a large fish with a shaved head like a Buddhist monk. The Hai Ho Shang is so strong and evil that it has been known to seize junks (Chinese boats) and drag them under water, often drowning their entire crew. There are two ways of getting rid of this disagreeable fish. One is by burning feathers, for it cannot stand the smell of that. This method was so successful that until quite recently travellers on the South China Seas never left the shore without taking a bag of feathers with them, just in case they met the dreaded monster-fish!

The other method of escape is by performing a special dance. As mermaids are drawn to the sound of music, so is the Sea Bonze, and provided the right dance was performed at the right time its ferocious temper could be soothed. Every ship was forced to carry a sailor who had been well trained in the steps of this dance and, as soon as a Sea Bonze was reported in the area, he would begin to perform it. To do it properly he needed to wear a long, black flowing gown with full sleeves. Another sailor would stand in the prow of the ship with a gong on which to beat out the rhythm of the dance. The dancing sailor would prance about on the deck waving a stick that had streamers of cloth tied to it. In almost every case the Hai Ho Shang ceased to cause trouble after the performance of the dance.

Although fully grown Sea Bonzes were thankfully rare, fishermen were said to pull in many nets filled with tiny Sea Bonzes who, when caught, would kneel before the fishermen and hold their feathery fins up as if praying for their lives. Unfortunately the fishermen were too afraid of them growing to full size and returning, so all had to be killed. The Chinese really believed that the Hai Ho Shangs were the sea bodies of drowned men who, instead of being able to rest in peace, were doomed to spend eternity luring fishermen to the same sort of death.

Hanuman the Ape

Hanuman is an ancient Indian god which has been worshipped for thousands of years and, in fact, is still worshipped today in the more primitive parts of India. His head is monkey-like but he has a human body and a cow's tail, and his body is green. He has a tribe of monkey followers who can come to his aid when necessary. He was said to be the son of the wind god Vayu and, according to legends, his mother was a nymph who had been turned into a monkey by a magic spell. Hanuman was swift, strong and very brave. When still a child he had attempted to leap up and touch the sun and, although not managing to reach it, he still leapt to a very great height in the sky – so high, in fact, that he frightened the sky god Indra, who threw a thunderbolt at him. It broke Hanuman's jaw and deformed his face, giving it an ape-like appearance.

The Harpy

The Harpy is a winged creature with the head and breasts of a woman and the body and talons of a vulture. In Greek legend

Harpies

the Harpies are noisy and ravenous, continually tormented with pangs of fierce hunger. They have long flowing hair which is matted, and filthy, like the rest of them, and they are deathly pale and thin from everlasting starvation. They are called the birds of hell. They swoop down from their mountain homes and devour any food they see, screeching and wailing to each other the whole time and giving off the most sickening smell. No one seems sure exactly how many Harpies there were, but we know of at least three. Their names were Aello, Ocypete, and Celano, and they were originally thought to be goddesses of the storm. In the British Museum in London there is a tomb which depicts the Harpies as demons of death who carry off the souls of the departed. Unfortunately, although permanently on the point of starvation themselves, they are unable to die or be killed.

Hecate

Hecate was said to be the goddess of the underworld and Queen of all witches. She was a figure much feared by the Greeks and the Romans. Hecate appeared only during the hours of darkness and was always followed by a pack of dogs. She prowled around graveyards and called up phantoms to frighten humans. Sometimes she would torment humans herself by shaking the earth and starting fires.

She had three faces; in the centre, that of a woman; on the right, that of a horse; and on the left, that of a dog. Images of Hecate were sometimes placed at crossroads, and often she was shown as having not only three faces, but three bodies as well. A three-bodied statue of her cast in bronze can be seen in the museum of Lyons in France. In hell she is said to guard all paths in and out and is a particular friend to sorceresses, who seek her help when mixing their philtres. A philtre is a magic potion to inspire or destroy love. It is made from nail

clippings, frog-bones, herbs, and fish, and is all mixed together with the blood of the loved one.

The Hippogriff or Hippogriffin

The Griffon was such a popular beast in the Middle Ages that it was hardly surprising it should give birth to another generation of amazing beasts. These were the Hippogriffs, the offspring of a Griffon (half-lion, half-Eagle) and an ordinary mare. The Hippogriff had a horse's body and tail combined with the claws, wings and beak of an eagle. This uncommon creature was apparently found only in mountain regions. The Hippogriff appears in legend quite late and belongs more to folklore and historical romance than to mythology.

The story of the most famous Hippogriff is told in detail by Ariosto in his epic poem *Orlando Furioso*. In this story a

Hippogriff was tamed by a magician named Atlantes. Atlantes had a foster-son, Rogero, whom he kept prisoner in a castle built for him by dwarves. The castle was on top of the Pyrenees and almost impossible to reach. Rogero was a valiant knight who had earned the title of hero whilst fighting for the King of Africa. Through his magical powers Atlantes could see into the future, and he knew his foster-son was destined to fall in love with a beautiful girl and be converted to Christianity. Atlantes, who worshipped the Devil, had no intention of allowing this to happen. The girl, whose name was Bradamante, was a female knight and she was just as determined that she would have Rogero for herself. Equipped with a magic ring which protected the wearer from all evil enchantments, she made her way to the castle and offered to fight the wizard, with Rogero as the prize.

Atlantes was delighted with this for, besides being mounted on a Hippogriff, he also possessed a shield which blinded all who looked upon it. As she was wearing her magic ring, Bradamante was unaffected by the blinding shield, but she fell to the ground and feigned death. The foolish Atlantes was lured into dismounting from the Hippogriff and Bradamante had no difficulty in overcoming him and forcing him to release Rogero. Bradamante gave Rogero the magic ring and together they passed through the castle gates, Bradamante on her horse and Rogero on foot. As they made their way down the mountain they discovered the Hippogriff grazing peacefully in the foothills. As he had no horse, the brave Rogero decided to try his luck with the Hippogriff and mounted it without difficulty.

It soared away at incredible speed, leaving poor Bradamante behind. The first bound took them to the top of the Pyrenees and the second one to Africa! Unfortunately, Rogero had no idea how to control the Hippogriff and it took many months and many adventures before he was able to return to his beloved Bradamante again.

Creatures from the Hollow Earth

The Old Ones

There are persistent legends in nearly every culture that tell of Old Ones, an ancient race of people who populated the earth millions of years ago. According to these legends, the Old Ones were tremendously intelligent and scientifically advanced and have now retreated to the caverns under the earth. There they manufacture their own necessities without needing to come to the surface – apart from those odd occasions, of course, when they emerge to kidnap human children to rear as their own.

In almost all the legends, the Old Ones have gone underground to escape natural catastrophes or the hidden death that lurks in the life-giving rays of sun. Some legends say that the Hollow Earth people have very long lives and have been joined by tribes from the lost city of Atlantis. Other stories say that these underground folk are colonies of space creatures who, after walking the earth for some hundreds of years, have now retired to underground bases to watch over the primitive species' intellectual and cultural development.

The Huldrefolk

The Huldrefolk (Norwegian for 'hidden people') live under the earth beneath hillocks and knolls and particularly in mountainous regions. They collect articles of silver and are generally thought to be rather wealthy. The Huldrefolk are very similar in appearance to ordinary folk, but slightly smaller. The only real giveaway, as far as the female Huldrefolk are concerned, are their hollow backs and cow's tails.

Although peaceable much of the time, Huldrefolk can be

treacherous and unpredictable and are best left to their own devices. There are many legends about children who have been snatched from their cradles and carried off to the mountains. There are also several disappearances of adult shepherds that have not been explained satisfactorily.

If Huldrefolk are your neighbours it might be prudent to remember that they are afraid of weapons made of steel or fire. They don't like to hear the name of Jesus very much, either.

The Hydra

The Hydra was a water serpent born to Echidna, a beautiful woman who was half-serpent herself. There was nothing in the least beautiful about the Hydra for, apart from her scaly, serpent-like body, she had many hideous human heads. No one ever agreed on the exact number; some said one hundred, some said fifty, but most people believed she had about nine. The probable reason for this confusion was that whenever one was cut off, two more sprouted in its place – making it difficult to keep track of how many the Hydra had at any one time! The head that sprouted in the middle was said to be immortal and so, in fact, the Hydra could never be killed.

This she-monster lived amongst the marshes near the lake of Lerna in a part of Greece once known as Argolis, where her breath, which was poisonous, turned the surrounding fields brown and dead and fouled the waters of the lake. Even when she slept the pollution in the air around her could easily cause a man to fall dead. She seemed set to cause havoc for eternity until Hercules came along. Hercules was the most famous of all Greek heroes. He was well known for his strength, endurance and courage in the face of overwhelming danger. A jealous goddess once sent two serpents to destroy him when he was a sleeping baby lying in his cradle. He was already so strong that he strangled the snakes with his tiny hands.

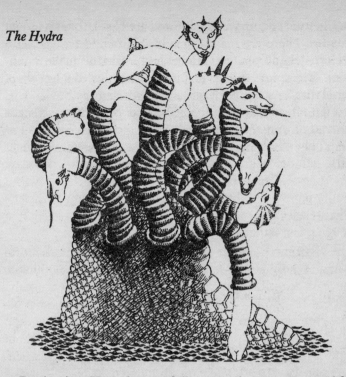

By the time Hercules was fully grown he was renowned for his feats of great strength and one day, on the instructions of the oracle, he went to serve King Eurystheus. The King told him he would give him ten difficult tasks to perform and if he completed them and survived he would become immortal like the gods, and therefore have everlasting life.

The tasks, needless to say, seemed impossible! The second of them was to destroy the many-headed Hydra. Hercules took with him on this adventure his trusty servant, Iolanus. This intrepid pair waded cautiously through the poisonous marshes to the place where the vile Hydra writhed and splashed in the murky water. By this time several men had been to lop off her heads so she already had a great deal more than she started with. Hercules set about the monster with arrows and a sword but as he lopped off one head, two more sprang up, spitting venom at their attacker with long forked tongues.

Hercules and Iolanus then made a fire on the marshes and, using their spears as branding irons, they burned the necks of the Hydra as soon as Hercules had severed the heads. This had the effect of sealing the necks and stopping more heads from sprouting. The severed heads were also burned immediately. The last head, which was deathless, Hercules buried under a great stone where it remains to this day, brooding and plotting. Hercules took some of the Hydra's deadly poison with him and used it to tip his arrows when he fought other evil creatures in the remaining tasks given him by King Eurystheus.

Iroquois Stonish Giants

The Iroquois tribe of Indians have many interesting folk tales about the North American lands on which they lived many years ago. The tales of their heroes and their monsters make interesting reading, particularly those of the Stonish Giants or *Ot-ne-yar-heh* which overran the country, fought many battles, and held the people in their power for a long time. It was said that the Stonish Giants began as a family of Indians who had become separated from the rest of the tribe at the Mississippi River. In a starving and desperate condition they had begun by eating their animals raw and eventually, when there were no more animals to be found, they began to invade other parts of the country. They practised rolling themselves in sand which, apparently, made their bodies very hard and caused them to grow into giants. One day the 'Holder of the Heavens', unhappy at the way they were behaving, led them into a great ravine and rolled stones over them in the night, but one escaped and went to live in the North.

The people of Onondagas have a different story; they say

that a stone giant lived just near their reservation. He was once just a normal man but he was greedy and gluttonous and eventually became a cannibal, which greatly increased his size. His skin became hard and grew scales tough enough to cause arrows to bounce off them. Every day when he walked through the valley he would catch and eat an Onondago, which naturally caused the people great distress. One day they made a road in the marshes with a covered pit and lured the giant along it. He fell into the man-trap and was killed. When the people pulled him out they were surprised to find that he was completely made of stone.

The Jenny Haniver

Whether or not many of the monsters in this book ever really lived we can never prove for certain, but amongst those we know which definitely could *not* have existed were what were called the 'Jenny Hanivers' actually man-made fakes. In the sixteenth and seventeenth centuries there was fantastic interest in monsters. Everyone believed that there were frightening beasts of one kind or another and it became the fashionable thing in certain circles to have one on display. According to the timeless rule of supply always meeting demand, hundreds of amazing monsters were created by greedy, dishonest people for the rich who desired them.

Apparently it was quite possible for a skilful, painstaking craftsman to make a creditable Dragon by adding to and subtracting from parts of a giant ray fish. Often, dried lizards with bat's wings attached to their bodies were sold as baby Dragons, and the Japanese were particularly good at fixing the tail of a fish to the upper part of a monkey or other small animal and selling it as a Mermaid. In many well-known museums there were such items as 'feathers from a Phoenix's tail', a unicorn's horn, and there were, of course, always plenty of stuffed Dragons, or rather, Jenny Hanivers!

Two very respectable and knowledgeable eighteenth century collectors had an unusual monster which they believed to be real. They were extremely proud of it and were delighted to show it to the famous Swedish naturalist Linnaeus when he called on them in Hamburg. He was thrilled with the monster, much to the satisfaction of the owners, but when they asked him what he thought were its best features he told them he thought it was the cleverest Jenny Haniver he had ever seen. It was made entirely, he claimed, from snakes' skins, weasels' teeth, birds' claws and many other unlikely things. The owners were furious, and Linnaeus was not only shown the door but threatened with prosecution for injuring their property. Rather surprised and shaken, the poor man left Hamburg immediately!

The Jinn

Allah created three different kinds of being, according to the Moslem religion – Angels, who are made of light; Men, who are made of earth; and the Jinn (the plural of Genie), who are made of fire. It is said that the Jinn were created from a black smokeless fire thousands of years before the creation of Adam. Apparently there are good and evil Jinn as well as male and female ones and they are aerial animals with transparent bodies that can take on various forms. At first they may appear as huge, swirling pillars of smoke which gradually compress into the form of a man, wolf, lion, scorpion, jackal or snake.

When they take on the shape of a man they are gigantic, and can be very handsome or very ugly but never anything in between. When they wish to, they can disappear into thin air or through a solid wall. They usually live in ruined houses, rivers and marketplaces. The Egyptians say that sandstorms are caused by the work of an evil Genie, and it seems they are always causing trouble of some kind or another. They throw bricks at passers-by from roofs and windows, they kidnap beautiful women, they steal food and haunt honest people who try to move into empty houses. One can usually get rid of them, however, by calling on the name of Allah.

Kappa

One of the most feared beasts in long-ago Japan was the 'river-child' or Kappa. It had the body of a tortoise, the legs and webbed feet of a frog and the head of a monkey. It had two other very unusual features. The first was its size, for although it weighed 9 kilograms (20 pounds), it was only 10 centimetres (4 inches) long. In spite of this apparent disadvantage it attacked grown men and devoured them; in fact even horses were said to have been dragged into its watery lair. The second strange thing about it was the shape of its monkey-like head. The whole of the top was hollowed out and filled with a special liquid which was said to be responsible for giving the monster its superhuman strength. Around the edge of the cavity was a thick fringe of red hair sticking out at angles like porcupine quills.

It was believed that one way of soothing a Kappa was to throw him cucumbers, a vegetable to which he was particularly partial. If that failed there was one sure way of escaping being eaten alive. Bow deeply to the Kappa. He is so polite that he will return your bow and as he does so the special liquid will spill from his head and he will lose his magic powers. While he is feeling weak, run in the opposite direction as quickly as possible!

One day, according to one old story, a horse that had gone down to a stream to drink ran back to the stable shaking with fear. When the groom investigated the reason for the horse's fright he discovered a tiny Kappa sitting on a lily pad. The horse created such a commotion that all the other servants, and even the master of the house, rushed out to see what was happening. They all bowed to the Kappa, as they had heard that this was the right thing to do, and the Kappa bowed back, spilling his magic fluid out on to the ground. Encouraged by his weakness the master, who happened to be a samurai, or fierce warrior, stepped forward and chopped off the Kappa's right arm. The weird little creature began to weep and begged for his life.

Kappa

The samurai, moved by the Kappa's sad plight, promised to set him free if he would write an apology to the horse and promise never to harm anyone again. The Kappa agreed, but asked for the return of his arm. This surprised the samurai, as the arm was obviously useless. The Kappa went on to explain that he could rub a healing ointment on it that would attach it to his body and make it perfectly normal again by morning. The warrior refused the arm until the Kappa had given him the secret formula for this amazing ointment. A bargain was struck and the Kappa was not seen again. Today the descendants of the samurai still sell a special medicine for the mending of broken limbs.

K'i-lin

The K'i-lin is really the Chinese version of the well-known western Unicorn, and it was first heard of as early as 2800 BC. To the Chinese, the K'i-lin is an animal of good fortune and is still loved by the people. They say that it is so gentle that when it walks it is careful not to tread on the tiniest living insect, and it will eat only dead grass rather than that which is alive and growing. It has the body of a large deer, the tail of an ox and the hooves of a horse. Its horn, which grows out of the middle of its forehead, is made of flesh and is shorter than that of the Western Unicorn. Its voice has the beautiful tone of a monastery bell. It makes its home in wild, remote places and cannot be captured. It is seen only on very rare occasions and its appearance is supposed to foretell the birth or death of a great king. The K'i-lin's life-span is a thousand years.

Early in the history of China, the K'i-lin is said to have appeared to the Emperor on the banks of the Yellow River. The Emperor, a wise and popular ruler, was very concerned about the future of his people and was taxing his brains for a way of passing his thoughts down to the next generation. Whilst he was sitting thinking, the K'i-lin came out of the river and approached the Emperor, Fu Hsi. On the back of the K'i-lin, Fu Hsi saw written what appeared to be strange magic signs. He studied them carefully and then copied them on to the shell of a tortoise, after which he fell into a deep sleep. When he awoke, the mysterious K'i-lin had vanished. Emperor Fu Hsi took the symbols back to his wise men at the palace and together they built up from them the first written language of China.

After this, the K'i-lin appeared several times, once in the palace grounds just before the death of the Yellow Emperor Huang Ti, and again before the deaths of some of the Emperors who followed him. After his visits to the early

Chinese Emperors the K'i-lin vanished for quite a long time. This was not really surprising, as by this time China was torn by civil wars. The sweet and gentle K'i-lin, the symbol of perfection, would never show himself at a time like this. It was not until the sixth century BC, many years later, that another visit from the K'i-lin was recorded. This time he appeared to a woman, a kind and good person, whose most desperate wish was to give birth to a son. One day as she was going to the temple to pray she trod by accident in the footprints of the K'i-lin and a piece of jade dropped at her feet. It had a carved inscription telling her that the son she would bear would be the next king, but without a throne. Her son was born a year later and is known to us today as Confucius, the greatest philosopher of China.

Soon after this the K'i-lin disappeared completely, apparently for ever. The Chinese people did not forget the sacred beast and every new emperor desperately hoped that he would show himself, if only for a moment. Finally, in the fifteenth century, a Chinese ship returned from East Africa carrying a weird and wonderful animal more or less answering the description of the K'i-lin. The Chinese people were delighted and hailed it as the Chinese Unicorn of ancient times. Today we call it the giraffe.

King Kong – the Man-Made Monster

Many times man has attempted actually to create the monsters of his imagination, often for his own gain, but never has one met with as much success as the giant gorilla, Kong, which caught the imagination of the world. In 1929 Merian C. Cooper, a maker of documentary films, went to Africa to shoot scenes for an adventure film and while he was out there he wrote a story which had for its central character a very large gorilla. Two years later, with a special effects expert called Willis O'Brien, he began to make the story into a film. O'Brien had a special way of making models more realistic. By shooting one frame, moving the models slightly, shooting another frame, moving the models again – over and over and with the greatest care – O'Brien finally got a film where the monster ran, jumped and fought to the death if required.

A 40-centimetre (16-inch) model of a gorilla was built for the film, and work began. It was a long, time-consuming job and after ten hours of work only 7½ metres (25 feet) of film were produced, enough for only thirty seconds on the screen! For the parts in the film where the heroine had to be held in the monster's hand, an ape-like hand 2½ metres (8 feet) long had to be built. *King Kong* was released in 1933 and was a fantastic success, holding audiences spellbound by its realism. The story of the film is rather slow-moving by today's standards, but once the action starts the monster looks very impressive indeed.

The story begins as a film producer sets off to the mysterious Skull Island off the coast of Africa, to film a strange creature rumoured to be living there. As soon as the film crew arrive they are attacked by the local natives, who try to sacrifice one of the white women to the monster. He appears, huge and terrifying, grabs the girl and lumbers off. From then on the film becomes breathtaking as the men chase Kong through unbelievable perils, even meeting, at one stage, some terrifying man-eating Dinosaurs! Eventually the monster is knocked out by sleeping-gas and the film producer takes him to New York to put him in an exhibition. Needless to say, the monster soon breaks his chains and is off on the rampage around New York, treading on trains and causing general panic everywhere. The great ape has apparently fallen in love with the girl from the film crew and somehow manages to track her to her hotel, where he peers in the window, nearly frightening her to death!

Kong grabs her as she screams and off they go again. The following morning finds the gorilla astride the top of the

Empire State Building (which, at the time the film was made, was the tallest building in the world). The climax of the story comes as fighter planes encircle the bewildered monster, pumping bullets into his body as he swats them like flies. Finally Kong begins to feel the pain of the bullets and, first putting the girl on a safe ledge, he falls to his death. *King Kong* is said to be the best film of its kind ever made, for not only did the monster appear real, he took on a personality of his own and came out of the film as the hero, not the villain, which had not been the film's first intention.

In the excitement of it all many people forgot that Kong was not real; he became almost a cult figure in America. Even today children who have never seen the film know the name 'King Kong'!

Kraken

The Kraken

In the early days before the sea had become the highway of the nations it is today, very little was known about the creatures who lived in it. Being too afraid of the sea's turbulent moods to do much investigating, the people who lived on its shores often let their imagination run riot.

One of the monsters steadfastly believed in was the Kraken, a mammoth sea monster often 2 kilometres (1½ miles) across, with many waving tentacles. The Kraken is famous in the legends of the Scandinavian coast. Norwegian fishermen claimed that when they went out fishing on hot

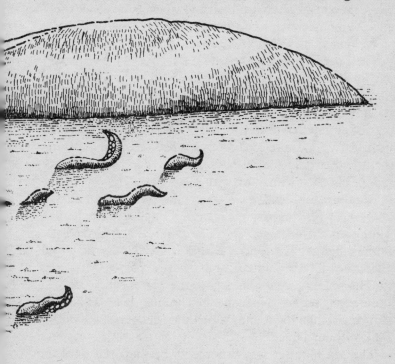

summer days they would sometimes find a depth of only twenty or thirty fathoms in a place which would normally be eighty or a hundred fathoms. They knew from this that a Kraken was lying at the bottom. This was always a happy omen for the fishermen, as the sea beast brought with it hosts of other small fish, and on Kraken days the fishermen filled their nets without any trouble at all. The monster was said to be quite harmless unless you happened to get in its way. One legend tells us of two fishermen who got their boat caught up in what they thought was a great mass of seaweed, but they soon realized it was the edge of a Kraken island. While they were stuggling to get away, one of the creature's vast arms brushed against their boat and almost wrecked it but, by a stroke of good luck, it knocked them back into a calm sea. They then managed to get their leaky boat back home safely and the monster made no attempt to interfere with them.

Writers in the Middle Ages tell us how a fully grown Kraken would sometimes rise to the surface of the water and anchor itself in one place. Shingle would be tossed on it by the sea and grass, and even bushes would eventually grow on it. It would stay there dozing until a boatload of sailors arrived, intending to stay the night. As soon as they landed, lit fires and began to cook food, the Kraken, angry at being disturbed, would plunge back into the depths, taking the sailors and their ship down with it.

Another story tells of a bishop who landed on a Kraken, and had a very narrow escape! One Sunday when he was sailing on a Norwegian ship he saw an island he had not noticed before. He decided that as it was Sunday he would claim the island in God's name and have a religious service on it. The sailors rowed him over to the island, where he held quite a long service. No sooner had he safely boarded his own ship again than the island, which was, of course, a Kraken, sank without a trace.

The sea monster was believed to be immortal until, in 1680, the body of one was caught in a narrow channel between the rocks and cliffs near a Norwegian village called Alstahong. It was an unusual happening, as the Kraken usually kept well away from the land. This poor thing had completely tangled its long tentacles in some trees by the shore and its body had become wedged fast in a cleft in the rock. The unfortunate beast had hung there in great discomfort until it died. It took a long time for its body to decay and until it did the awful smell made the narrow channel impassable!

The Great Dog Ku of Hawaii

Hawaiian legends often unite human and animal forms into one complete being, rather like the Centaurs of Roman mythology. A frightening example is the shark-man who, because his vast mouth is placed between his shoulder blades, is forced to wear a cloak to conceal his deformity. The legend of the great dog Ku is slightly different, as he had the power to turn himself into a man or back into an animal whenever he wished.

One day, Ku the dog-man decided to visit mankind, so he took on the shape of a very small dog and appeared on a sunny beach near the home of an important chief. Here, Na-pihe-nui, the chief's daughter, and several of her handmaidens came down every day to bathe. One of the girls was diving from a shelf on a rocky ledge when she saw something moving on the shore. She called to her friends and they rushed over to the place where they had left their clothes. A tiny white dog was lying on the princess's cloak. The girls were delighted with him as he joined in their fun in the water, and it soon became clear that he had become very attached to the princess. When the maidens returned home they took the frisky little dog with them. The girl's father was not so easily taken in by the dog and regarded his sudden appearance with suspicion. Somehow he found out about the dog's ability to turn himself into a man, and he became very frightened. He ordered his servants to kill the dog, but once Ku realized what was about to happen he escaped into the woods. He was very angry about the way he had been treated and decided to carry the princess away as his wife.

He turned himself into a handsome, well-dressed man and went to the chief's home to ask for the princess's hand in marriage, but the chief refused him. Ku was even more angry and threatened to kill all the chief's people, but the chief only drove him away. The next morning when the chief looked over the mountains he saw an enormous fierce dog coming out of a cave on the mountainside. His heart sank and he realized that he had made a very powerful enemy indeed. His worst fears were justified when he heard that Ku was catching his people one by one and devouring them.

The chief took all the womenfolk in his family, including the princess, and hid them in a cave with plenty of food and water. Stones were placed in front of the opening so that the enemy would have difficulty in finding the women. The chief gathered his followers around him and together they launched an attack on the great dog Ku. It was a hard struggle, as Ku was very strong and devoured many people during the fighting. Finally, after many prayers to the gods, Ku was overpowered and beaten to the ground. When he was dead his body was cut into two pieces which were thrown a long way away from each other. The chief's priests turned the pieces into the two great stones that have been objects of great interest to the Hawaiians for many years.

Ku still appears today in Hawaii, usually in cloud formations on top of the great mountains, where he can be seen stretching from one peak to another above the cave which is his home.

Kujata

Kujata is a monster god from ancient Moslem mythology. He is a vast bull with four thousand eyes, ears, nostrils, mouths and feet, and it would take five hundred years to travel from one eye to another and from one ear to another. It is said that on the bull's back there is a giant ruby on top of which there stands an angel who touches our earth. Kujata the bull himself stands on the back of a fish, under which roars a mighty sea. Under the air there is fire, and under the fire there is a mighty serpent large enough to swallow the whole universe!

The Laidley Worm of Lambton

In the Middle Ages, reports of Dragon-slaying became almost an everyday occurrence and it was said that there was a time when nobody was anybody unless hey had killed a Dragon. Among the many British Dragon legends one of the earliest and best known is that of the Laidley Worm of Lambton, in the north-east of England, which was killed in a very unsporting manner by the young heir of Lambton. In his younger days the boy used to spend his Sundays fishing in the River Wear. One day he found on his hook a tiny worm, which he tossed away without a second thought. In an amazingly short time this worm grew until it was the size of an enormous Dragon. It used to lie every day in the sun on the banks of the River Wear, coiled around itself nine times. It soon began to terrorize the villagers, demanding the milk from nine cows daily, and if anyone forgot to deliver the milk it devoured instead the first man or animal that crossed its path. Whilst all this was going on the heir was busy overseas

fighting in the Crusades. When he eventually returned he was horrified to hear what had been happening in his absence and decided that God must have created the monster to punish him for fishing on Sundays (which was very much frowned on in those days!)

He volunteered at once to slay the horrible beast, but every time he attacked it and cut it in half the two pieces joined up again. Finally he asked the advice of a witch, who told him to use a coat of armour studded with razor-edged blades when next he went to see the Dragon. The young man did as she told him and, wearing the deadly suit of armour, went and stood on the rock in the middle of the river. The serpent rushed at him in a temper and wound itself around the knight nine times. It was soon cut into many, many pieces which were washed away by the river.

The Lamias

Among the myths of Rome and Greece are the stories of the Lamias, which were said to live in Africa. They were beautiful women from the waist upwards but writhing serpents from the waist downwards. They were greatly feared, sometimes as witches and sometimes as monsters. They were unable to speak but could make a beautiful whistling noise in order to lure lost travellers to a place where the Lamias could devour them.

The first Lamia on record was said to be the beautiful Queen of Libya, who was greatly loved by the Greek god Zeus. The most wonderful gift he could think of to give her was the power to pluck out people's eyes and replace them at will! When Zeus's wife Hera (who also happened to be his sister!) found out about this passion for another woman, she had all Lamia's children murdered. Lamia's fury and bitterness caused her to take on the shape of a serpent woman and for ever after to eat every child that crossed her path. She even had the ability to spirit babies from the wombs of pregnant women.

Lemures

Lemures were the souls of dead people who sometimes decided to come back to earth to reunite themselves with their bodies. The Etruscans and Romans took them very seriously and thought that the Lemures also attached themselves to living people in order to torment them. To appease the Lemures strange ceremonies known as 'The Lemuria' were conducted regularly every May. The father of each family would offer black beans to the demons to pacify them. It was rumoured at one time that they were a type of Vampire, but apparently this was disproved. They were just spirits who enjoyed making a nuisance of themselves.

The Loch Ness Monster

Loch Ness, in Northern Scotland, holds the key to one of the world's oldest and most baffling mysteries. Reports on the elusive Monster said to live in this forbidding stretch of water are to be found in our newspapers at least once or twice a year, and you can be sure that there is always one Monster-hunting expedition lurking around the loch with long-range telescopes! The strange legend of the Great Worm, Water Horse or Kelpie (just a few of its many names) goes very far back into history. The fact that there are so many water-monster stories in Scottish folklore may be due to the fact that most of the Scottish Highlanders lived near areas of deep water and, because it was part of their life, took a great deal of interest in it. On the other hand, it could have been something a lot more sinister! The Kelpie of folklore turns up in different shapes and colours and in different places, but the Great Water Horse of Loch Ness was said to be particularly large and black!

We have to go back as far as the sixth century for the first written report of a sighting of the Monster by St Columba, an early Christian missionary preaching to the pagan tribesmen in the Highlands of Scotland. While he was working up there he found it necessary to cross the River Ness, and when he arrived safely at the bank he found some of the local people burying a poor man who had been attacked by the water

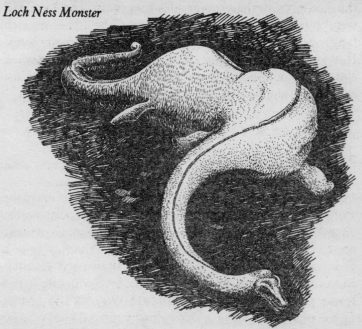

monster and savagely bitten to death. St Columba then told his companions to swim out and bring in the dead man's boat. One of them undressed and jumped into the water but the Monster which had been hiding on the bottom, swam up to the surface and chased the man with its mouth wide open. St Columba made the sign of the Cross and shouted to the ferocious beast, telling it to go away. The Monster, startled at being shouted at by a priest, quickly made off in the opposite direction!

The water monster was reported occasionally in the centuries that followed but the Highlanders were remote, secretive people and there may have been many glimpses of the Monster that were neither talked about nor written down. Loch Ness itself was desolate and lonely and in fact very few people passed by it, because the thin path around it was so winding and difficult to walk on.

In 1933, however, things began to change, when work began on a new road from Inverness to Fort Augustus. This road was large enough to carry cars and lorries and passed close to the side of the Loch. Loch Ness itself is really a long narrow lake, 2-3 kilometres (1-2 miles) wide and about 40 kilometres (24 miles) long, forming part of the Caledonian Canal. In the Ice Age it was filled with glaciers, which gave it steep sides and a very flat bottom about 200 metres (700 feet) below the surface. The bottom is covered by a thick layer of mud and slime.

At the same time as the work started on the new road, something curious began to happen. People who were working around the loch at the time began to see a series of strange 'things' apparently swimming just below the surface of the water and leaving behind a large V-shaped backwash. On a sunny afternoon in May 1933 a Mr and Mrs McKay were driving along the north shore of the loch when Mrs McKay saw a large disturbance in the water. At first she thought it must be some wild ducks fighting, but as she watched the disturbance got bigger until two large black humps broke the surface one behind the other. She watched for several minutes as the humps swam out to the pier and then, with more splashing and wallowing, they disappeared from view. Mr McKay stopped the car in time to see the waves that the creature had made come rolling on to the shore.

The newspaper soon got hold of the story, and it caused a great deal of exitement. Many people came forward and told similar accounts of things they had seen in the loch. Another couple, a Mr and Mrs Spicer, claimed to have seen the Monster actually out of the water and lumbering about on the road. As they drove towards it, it flopped back into the loch and swam away. Mr Spicer, when describing it later, said that it seemed to have a long neck which moved up and down like a scenic railway and looked like pictures he had seen of prehistoric animals. By 1934 excitement was really mounting. A veterinary student caught sight of the Monster from his motorbike. He said it had a large thick body with two front flippers and two others behind, apparently webbed. He said that it was about 6 metres (20 feet) long. A passing chemist from Inverness was alarmed by its huge neck and strong, threshing tail. Money prizes were offered for the capture of a real, live Loch Ness Monster and Bertram Mills offered £20,000 for one to use in his circus!

To most people in Britain it seemed pretty well established that the much-talked-about loch contained at least one huge, long creature with several humps, a swanlike neck and a long, powerful tail. In spite of its size and terrifying appearance, however, the Monster was supposed to be peaceful and timid. Whenever it was spotted it was either swimming quietly in the loch or sunbathing on the shore. It soon disappeared at the sight or sound of humans and there is certainly no modern record of it attacking anybody. Eventually, in July 1934, a twenty-man team of observers were posted on all sides of the loch between 9 a.m. and 6 p.m. every day for a period of twelve weeks. Twenty-one photographs were taken, also a 3-metre (10-foot) length of moving film. This evidence was shown to a team of scientists who, to everyone's amazement, decided that the Monster was probably just a large, grey seal! They didn't go on to explain how a seal could have got in the loch in the first place.

This discouraging news put an end to any further Monster-hunting expeditions and very few sightings were reported. Then in 1939 World War II broke out and people turned their minds to other things. There just wasn't room in the papers any more for stories of monsters. It was quite a long time after the war ended in 1945 before most people could afford to take holidays, and it wasn't really until the mid-fifties that Scotland's tourist trade began to be healthy again. With the influx of visitors came fresh reports of vast, dark shapes swimming in Loch Ness and of disturbances in the water and large V-shaped backwashes. Some people even managed to take pictures, although it was surprising how many reported that their camera just didn't work at the right moment, or found later, when the film was developed, that it showed hardly any of what the watcher thought he saw. A lot of this 'voodoo' was probably due to the fact that the lighting was always bad around the loch and shots often had to be taken great distances away from the mysterious creature.

One family, called Lowrie, were in a yacht passing through the loch when they saw and photographed a large beast coming to the surface only 38 metres (40 yards) away from them. As they found the beast so large and so close to them they did not stop to take more pictures but turned and made for the shore. In one of these pictures a very clear V-shaped wake can be seen, but unfortunately there is no sign of the brown and green neck and humps the Lowries saw.

In 1960 Tim Dinsdale, a well-known and dedicated Monster-hunter, took a film of the Monster that was shown on television and seen by about five million people. Although the film was not very clear it did serve to stir up a great deal more interest in the Monster.

In 1964 two special viewing platforms were built by the Loch Ness Investigation Bureau and placed one on either side of the loch. Three long-range cameras were fixed on each, one movie camera and two still cameras. The person who was on lookout duty watched through a telescope that had a cross-hair lens, like that of a telescopic rifle. When the watcher got the Monster in his sights, all he had to do was press a trigger and the cameras rolled into action! The rigs were manned from Whitsun to October but in all that time there were only fifteen really fine warm days (the Monster was only ever seen on days like this) and when the creatures did appear they were always too far away to get a really clear film.

The last twenty years have seen an increase in the number and sophistication of investigations in Loch Ness. Small submarines have been used in experiments but unfortunately the water proved too murky and peat-stained for any photographs to be taken. The most interesting results up to now seem to have come with the use of sonar (echo-sounding) equipment. A sonar expedition in 1962 found a strong echo from a large unidentified object off Urquhart Castle on 20 July. The results of the various experiments carried out by this team proved beyond a doubt that there *were* large moving objects in the loch, certainly enough fish for them to feed on and wide ridges in the steep sides of the loch to harbour these massive creatures if they existed.

Since then there have been several scientific expeditions, of which those organized by Dr Robert Rines have been the most productive and interesting. In 1972 his sonar equipment picked up moving targets up to thirty times the size of salmon, and with the help of computers produced photographs which became the subject of wide discussion in the newspapers. The best known of these is the 'flipper picture' obtained 14 metres (42 feet) below the surface of Urquhart Bay on the night of 8 August 1972. It clearly shows an object 'about 9 metres (27 feet) long with projections or humps'. It has been suggested that the photograph shows either a paddle-like limb of considerable size or possibly a rhomboidal tail lobe of the kind developed by some of the Plesiosaurs.

Once again many people have remained unconvinced, mainly because the photographs were not quite clear enough. What is really needed now is a modern full-colour film of this bashful beast with close-ups of its profile! Several interesting books on the Monster have been written, which you might like to dip into. All of them have a selection of intriguing photographs. The following books can be obtained in most bookshops and libraries:

The Story of the Loch Ness Monster by Tim Dinsdale (published by Target).

Loch Ness Monster by Tim Dinsdale. Fourth edition (published by Routledge and Kegan Paul).

The Makara

The Makara, another name for sea monster, is a weird elusive creature which appears in the myths of both Buddhist and Hindu religions. Its appearance is so changeable that almost any unusual beast can be called a Makara. The only feature necessary for it to be a complete Makara is that one half should be fish and one half mammal; apart from that any combination is quite acceptable.

The Hindus have at least two variations of the Makara. Probably the best-known one has the body of a tortoise combined with an elephant's head and a fish's tail. The elephant's head has a great snout which curls back over enormous, bared teeth. There is also a scorpion's sting in the fish's tail. This unlikely creature was said to have been ridden by Ganga, the goddess of the holy river of India. She used to ride down the river on the Makara, spreading fertility and good fortune to the people who came to her shores to bathe.

Another Hindu Makara has a fish body and tail and the head and front legs of an antelope. It is thought that this particular Makara might be related to the goat-fish Capricorn, the tenth sign of our zodiac. In other Hindu folk tales, the Makara appears as an enormous crab whose mission was to protect fish from the birds and fishermen who preyed on them. It is impossible to travel far in the East today without coming upon the face of the Makara. Its features, elephant's head, snout and all, have become a popular decoration used in Indian and other Asian architecture.

The Manticora

Of all the weird animals supposedly related to man there is none so strange as the Manticora. In one version of Greek mythology it is described as having a head like a man's, with pale blue eyes and three rows of teeth which fit into each other like the teeth of a comb. The face and ears are bright red and it has a lion's body with a scorpion's tail with stings on either side which it can shoot off like arrows. It moves very swiftly and its voice resembles the combined sound of the flute and the trumpet. It is very, very fond of human flesh.

In a further description it is said to have twisted talons like drills and a great many darts in its tail which it shoots out at all angles. When it does so the trees it hits drip blood.

Medusa and the Gorgons

The Gorgons were three snake-haired women whose looks were so terrible that anyone who looked at them turned to stone. Medusa, the most fearsome of the Gorgons, had once been one of the loveliest maidens in Greece but unfortunately she had boasted that her own beauty was greater than that of the goddess Athene. The powerful Athene was angry and took her revenge by turning Medusa's lovely face into that of a hideous monster. Her tongue lolled from her mouth, her eyes glared and her teeth became sharp and pointed. Her lovely golden hair was changed into snakes which coiled about her head, constantly writhing and hissing. Like the rest of the Gorgons, who were her sisters, she turned to stone anyone who set eyes on her.

Another famous Greek hero, Perseus, promised to kill Medusa and take her head back as a gift to the cruel King

Polydectes. Before setting out on this mission, Perseus went to the temple of Athene and prayed to the goddess for help. Athene, still anxious to get rid of Medusa, decided to help him. She told him always to keep his back turned on the monster and to take care never to look into her face. To help him she gave him a highly polished shield to use as a mirror. Hermes, the messenger of the gods, also gave him a pair of winged sandals with which to fly over land and sea. He was then told to go to the Underworld, where he would obtain a strong, curved sword, a magic goatskin bag and a helmet of invisibility.

Medusa

After some time Perseus found his way down to the dark river of death, the Styx, where he found the maidens who guarded Athene's treasures. They regarded Perseus with suspicion but handed over the things he asked for and directed him to the place where Medusa lived. Perseus flew on until he came to a place where stood the shapes of many men now turned into stone! Among them lying asleep, he found Medusa. Her body was still like that of a young girl but her head was covered with a hundred serpents who squirmed and hissed as Perseus approached. Although Perseus only saw Medusa's reflection in the shield, he shuddered!

Hovering over her, he struck off her head with a blow of his mighty sword and, raising the Gorgon's head by its snaky locks, he thrust it into the goatskin bag. Although the other Gorgons awoke and chased him, he was protected by his helmet of invisibility and returned home with the Gorgon's head safely tied in his goatskin bag. A picture of Perseus escaping with Medusa's head and being pursued by her immortal sisters can be seen on a vase in the British Museum in London.

Mermaids and Mermen

The Mermaid is a romantic and mysterious creature who is known to us all. Always beautiful, usually unhappy, she is a woman down to her waist. Below there she has a scaly fish-tail. Her hair is usually waist-length, sometimes green, sometimes golden, and she is very often shown sitting on a rock combing her hair and gazing into a hand mirror. She has a beautiful voice and, on still moonlit nights, her haunting, hypnotic song is said to have lured many ships to their doom on the rocks near where she is sitting. When she is angry and unhappy, which is often, her howling can turn the sunniest day, into a raging tempest which can lash the boats of unsuspecting sailors on to the rocks. She has even been seen to do a wild dance on the tops of the waves during a storm.

Music has a strong appeal for the Mermaid, and she has often been known to come ashore to join in a dance in the village hall. She always wears a long dress, of course, and the hem of it is usually wet.

Up to the seventeeth century there was a strong belief in the Mermaid in both Eastern and Western countries. She was very often to be found in medieval heraldry on tiles used for floor-paving and on stone- and wood-carving in many places, including churches. She was very often painted or carved on ships, sometimes used as a figure-head, and was often to be seen painted on swinging inn-signs. The most famous inn she gave her name to, in 1603, was the Mermaid Tavern in Broad Street, London, which was said to have been used by Shakespeare, Ben Jonson and other well-known writers of that period.

Mermaid

It is possible that the legend of the Mermaid might have been begun by someone giving an exaggerated description of a sea-cow. One particular species, a dugong, sometimes raises the upper part of its body and looks around in an uncannily human way. The female gives birth to only one baby at a time and carries it under her fin in the same way that a human mother might tuck her baby under her arm. Perhaps early sea travellers caught a glimpse of this animal and helped to spread the word.

92

There are, however, records of creatures, half-human, half-fish, as far back as 1800BC, and on a seal-stone of that period the great Babylonian water god Ga is pictured standing on a goat-fish and on a Mermaid. There are legends of fish-gods from many other parts of the world; all of them seemed to be kindly, with the interests of the people at heart.

One interesting tale is told by the North American Indians. In the beginning they lived in a barren land on the Asiatic coast, where they were always hungry and cold. A Merman began to appear daily, swimming near the shore and singing to the people in his beautiful sea voice. The Merman looked like a man from the waist up but instead of legs he had two fish-tails joined together – which was considered unusual, even for a Merman. His hair and beard were very long and dark green, almost like seaweed. His haunting songs told them of wonderful lands where they could find food and live a contented life across the sea. He promised to guide them there if they put their trust in him. The Indians were naturally very suspicious, but as they were so near to starvation anyway they decided to take a chance. They built boats for themselves and, gathering up the last of their food, they embarked on the long voyage from Asia in the wake of the odd green-haired man-fish. They finally arrived on what turned out to be the shores of North America, where they settled and lived happily until their land was invaded by Europeans.

The stories of Mermen and Mermaids are endless and fascinating. At one time it was thought that Mermaids were heavenly fish-maidens who visited earth every so often to perform a ritual dance. Dancing has a special significance in folklore and different dances were said to bring success in hunting, in wars and in the bearing of fine, healthy children. All the stories of the dancing Mermaids have one thing in common. The Mermaid always takes off one of her garments, usually a cloak or a hat, in order to perform the dance. The garment is always stolen by a mortal, which means that the poor Mermaid is unable to go back to the land she came from and must remain on earth for ever.

There are stories of Japanese fishermen stealing the garments of the Mermaid. In Germany and Scandinavia the Mermaids were said to lose cloaks made of feathers or sealskin in exactly the same way. Often in these stories the mortal who steals the cloak marries the Mermaid but usually the stories end unhappily for the man, when the Mermaid finds her garment and leaves him in order to return to her sisters in the sea.

During the last two or three hundred years the Mermaid has become a much lonelier creature, always attempting to befriend the sailors of passing ships and following the sound of the music that she loves so much.

A sad story about the relationship between a Mermaid and a prince is told by Hans Andersen. The Mermaid fell in love with a prince whom she had saved after his ship was wrecked. In order to stay with him on land she sold her voice to a witch in exchange for a pair of legs. She knew, however, that if she wanted to stay with the prince, human legs were not enough – she needed his complete love, otherwise she would die. Although the prince liked her a lot, he was already in love with a princess and, on the morning of his marriage, the Mermaid threw herself back into the sea and was transformed into a spirit of the air.

There are many records of Mermaids being sighted, even quite recently. The famous explorer Henry Hudson (1570-1611) talked of how he and his whole ship's company once saw a Mermaid, and described her as being exactly like a woman with a speckled tail like a mackerel. In 1653 a party of fifty Dutch soldiers saw two Mermen swimming near a beach in broad daylight on two separate occasions. In 1673 a Mermaid was seen standing in the sea for two and a half hours by many people on the Faroe Islands. Interest in the Mermaid continued through the eighteenth century and bogus Mermaids were exhibited all over the country. They drew in the crowds and made money for their owners. In 1836 two showmen were quarrelling in court over the owner-ship of a Mermaid they had exhibited in the West End of London. On further investigation this particular Mermaid was found to be made out of the skin of a monkey stuffed, varnished and attached to the tail and body of a salmon!

The Minotaur

The Minotaur – as far as we know there was only one – was a hideous creature of Greek legend said to be the son of Queen Pasiphaë of Crete and a beautiful white bull that Neptune had brought from the sea. Poseidon (Neptune) had sent the bull to King Minos as a sacrifice, but the King refused to kill it. Poseidon was so insulted that he put a spell on Pasiphaë to make her fall in love with the bull. When the Queen's child was born it had the head and horns of a bull and the body of a man and was so hideous to look at that the Queen had a special maze constructed to house the monster. The maze, or labyrinth, was so cunningly and cleverly constructed that once installed inside it, the Minotaur could not hope to find its way out. In the same way anyone else who had the mis-fortune to be sent into it had no hope of ever escaping. The Minotaur refused to eat anything but human flesh so Minos, the King of Crete, had to find living humans to send into the labyrinth to appease him.

The people of Crete had recently been at war with the people of Athens and the warships of King Minos did so much damage to their country that King Aegeus of Athens was forced to beg for peace. King Minos eventually agreed to leave them alone, provided that every spring seven youths and seven girls were sent to Crete as food for the Minotaur. So every spring the fourteen young people were chosen by lot and sent in a ship with black sails to King Minos; so spring, usually a time of hope and new beginnings, was dreaded by the Athenians as a time of grief and mourning. When Theseus, the son of King Aegeus, returned to Athens from some adventure abroad, he was horrified by these human sacrifices and in spite of his father's pleas he decided to join the next boatload of young people to go out to Crete, in the hope of killing the Minotaur.

Aegeus was heartbroken, for he felt sure his son had no chance of succeeding, but, as a special favour, he asked Theseus to change his black sails for white ones if he should

Minotaur

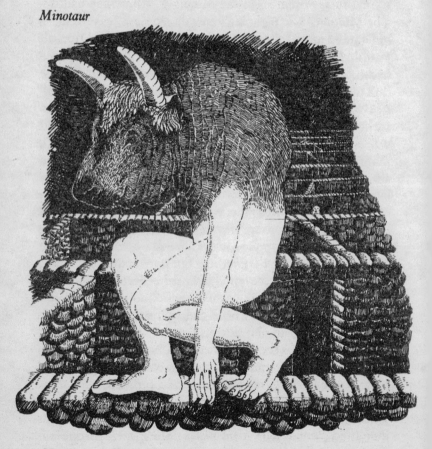

successfully return. Then, on the voyage home, Aegeus could look out for him over the cliffs and know by the colour of the sails whether his dear son was alive or dead.

It was a sad day when the boat sailed, and many tears were shed by the relatives of the young people, but Theseus refused to be downhearted. King Minos met the party of Athenians when they arrived in Crete and escorted them to his palace, where they were given a lavish banquet and allowed to stay the night. At this banquet, however, Ariadne, the King's daughter, fell in love with Theseus and was determined to save him from the Minotaur. After they had finished eating, she took him on one side and gave him an enchanted sword and a ball of wool. She explained that the sword would kill the Minotaur but they would need the wool to lay a trail in order to find their way out of the labyrinth.

The next morning Theseus and his companions were taken to the great bronze door of the maze and, once inside, the door was firmly locked behind them. Theseus then told the others about his plan for killing the Minotaur and begged them to stay hidden near the entrance of the maze. Theseus then fastened the end of the ball of wool to the doorpost and carefully unrolled it as he crept through the labyrinth. He had almost got to the end of the ball of wool when he heard a horrible snorting noise. Suddenly, from around the next corner, leapt the most hideous monster Theseus had ever imagined. The beast's great shaggy head, huge horns and wild flashing eyes were enough to make Theseus quake and tremble in his shoes. As he stood rooted to the ground, the beast lowered its mighty head and charged at him. Theseus managed to leap to one side and, as he did so, plunged his magic sword into the bull's neck. Although the beast continued to fight for some time, it was weakened by its wound and soon fell dead to the ground.

Theseus quickly grabbed the ball of wool and began to wind it up again as fast as he could until he reached his delighted companions at the door of the maze. Ariadne was also waiting for them with the key to the great bronze doors. The young Athenians rushed down to the harbour, taking Ariadne with them.

Meanwhile, in Athens, the King and all his people were waiting expectantly for news of Theseus. Aegeus stood hour after hour looking out for the sails of the Athenian boat. Finally the ship did appear over the horizon but the prince, in his excitement, had forgotten the promise he made to his father and had left the black sails billowing in the wind instead of the white ones. Aegeus was so overcome with grief when he saw the black sails that he rushed to the edge of the cliff and threw himself into the sea. Since that day the sea in which the King drowned has been called the Aegean. So, Theseus's triumphant voyage ended tragically. After the mourning period was over he was crowned King of Athens. There is a very old vase in the British Museum in London that shows the ball of wool scene from the labyrinth.

The Monster of Loch Garten

In the midst of the Abernathy Forest in the Highlands of Scotland lies lovely Loch Garten, its shores surrounded by birch trees and pine woods. According to tradition the part of it that flows through thick woods was haunted by a large, flesh-eating water monster. This ugly creature, a cross between a horse and a bull, had a jet-black mane, vast head and burning eyes. Its spine-chilling roar echoed around the hills at night and it satisfied its hunger on children and lambs.

Local legend tells us that a crofter decided to capture the beast and one day tied the end of a long rope around a large boulder weighing many tonnes and put it on the shore of Loch Garten. On the other end of the rope he tied a hook with a young lamb on it. He rowed the baited end of the giant fishing-line out into the middle of the loch and, after weighting it, dropped it over the side into the inky depths of the loch.

That night there was a tremendous storm which lashed and tore at the surface of the water. In spite of the noise of the thunder and the rain the angry sound of the Monster's fiendish snarling could be heard for miles around. The following morning the crofter went down to the shore to see if his trap had worked. All he could see was a deep groove in the sand leading to the water's edge where the great rock had been gradually pulled into the water. The loch is very deep and the Monster has not been seen or heard of ever since.

The Nagas

The story of the Nagas belongs to the mythology of India. The Nagas is one of the strangest of mythical monsters for it is half-god, half-human, yet it always takes the body of a snake. It possesses great wealth and very strange powers that no one really understands. People dreaded and feared it because they thought it could cause or prevent rain which, of course, meant life or death to the Indian people. The Naga is to India and South-East Asia what the Dragon is to China, and is often used as a decoration on palaces and temples. Often a pilgrim to these countries would be greeted by the image of a pair of Nagas, each with seven heads forming a hood like that of a cobra, flanking the shrine he was visiting.

The Naga has supreme power over water – the rivers, the seas and the rain – and can create good or evil from it according to the way he feels on that particular day. Nagas live in great splendour, either under the earth or at the bottom of the rivers and oceans. Like many mythical monsters, they live in sumptuous palaces overflowing with gold and precious jewels. In the throat or forehead of every Naga a priceless jewel is worn, and it is this that is said to give them their magic powers.

The timeless Indian fear of drought was always closely linked to the Nagas, and there are many stories woven around them to show that despite their mischief-making they were still very important to human life. One story is about a magician who wished to test the strength of his magic against the magic of the Nagas. He somehow captured all the Nagas and sealed them in a cave with a magic seal. There are gods who protect the Nagas, however, and they sent a beautiful girl to try to tempt the magician. As soon as he saw her he fell in love with her and by doing so lost all his magic powers. His spell no longer held the Nagas imprisoned in their cave and they broke free. As they flew into the sky, rain began to fall and put an end to the long days of drought.

The female Nagas are called Naginis and are usually charming and beautiful creatures. Yet, like Mermaids and other semi-human creatures, they have a weakness for mortal men and often fall in love with them. The marriage of a Nagini and a human prince was supposed to have been responsible for the creation of the country of Cambodia (Kampuchea), or so legend has it.

In India, there is still strong belief in the Nagas and some Indian tribes claim to be related to or descended from these weird spirits. With the march of civilization the Nagas appear less often, but they can still be found by a chosen few, lurking in shallow pools and streams and, of course, there must be many more to be found under the great rivers and seas. These Nagas often resemble very ordinary snakes, but, knowing as we do of their supernatural powers, we should treat them with great respect if we should meet them face to face!

The Nandi Bear

Today in East Africa there is a wild beast called the Nandi Bear or, in the language of the people, the Chemosit. It is named after the Nandi tribe, who strongly believe in it today, and there are many men who claim to have seen it or heard its hideous cry, a sound so evil that it can never be forgotten. It is not just the tribespeople who have heard the cry of the Chemosit; hunters from many different countries, and even zoologists making scientific studies of the animals in that particular area, have heard it.

The tracks of this giant bear have often been seen and its footprints are four times the size of a man's, with three claws on each foot. It is called a bear because the footprints look like those of bears, but there have never been bears in this part of the world before! The people of the Nandi tribe believe that the bear is the devil come down in human form. For its food it eats only people! Apparently it is particularly fond of human brains, and some Africans in isolated parts of the country still wear baskets on their heads when crawling out of their huts to ward off attack on their heads by the wandering Chemosit.

The Elgayo tribe, who were reputed to be fearless hunters and trackers, until recent years wore straw helmets when they went out hunting. The mothers of the tribe threaten their children with the Nandi Bear and tell them it is a bogeyman that will come and snatch them away if they are naughty!

It is sometimes said to be a one-legged monster, half-man, half-bird, with a mouth that shines a luminous red at night. Many people who have actually caught glimpses of this terrifying creature, usually whilst moving hurriedly in the opposite direction, say that it sits on its haunches like a dog and seems to be covered with long shaggy hair. It is obviously an animal of the night, for no one reports seeing it in daylight and its eerie cry is never heard before sundown.

An interesting story was once told by an engineer called Angus McDonald, who went out to Africa to work on some land development. He and his fellow-workers were living in a camp in Kenya near the site were he was working. The nearest civilized place was a hundred miles away. He slept in a primitive hut called a *banda*, where his bed was placed alongside the window. One night he was awakened by a noise directly underneath the window and, when he got out of bed to investigate, a great hairy body leapt through the window and knocked him to the ground. As it did so the creature gave a piercing scream of rage quite unlike any animal he had ever heard in his life.

McDonald managed to break free but the hairy thing proceeded to chase him around the hut, smashing and breaking things as it went. As far as he could tell, as it was rather dark, the thing travelled on two legs, and it bumped into him several times while chasing him in and out of the hut. McDonald's three dogs had been outside the hut but they had run off, howling in terror. Their panic-stricken barking soon roused the whole camp, and pandemonium broke out as the other engineers began banging tins and sceaming to frighten the raider away. After five minutes the creature charged out of the hut, leaving it almost completely wrecked. McDonald told his workmates later that the creature had uttered its blood-curdling scream with a wide-open mouth. In the dark its mouth seemed to glow bright red. He thought it was about 2 metres (7feet) tall, ape-like and with a strong mouldy smell.

The next morning the animal's footprints could be clearly seen. They were round and bear-like and ended in toes. McDonald got a party of men together to try to track it down but the two Elgayo tribesmen they had with them, previously noted for their bravery, refused to go. They said they could still smell something terrifying, and it could only be the dreaded Chemosit.

The Nasnas

This unfortunate creature is
said to be half a human being,
with half a head, half a body,
one arm and one leg on which it
hops. It is also able to speak. It
is found in the woods and desert
country of the Yemen. One
version of the Nasnas says it has
its face in its chest and a sheep's
tail, whilst another says it has
the wings of a bat and lives near
the China seas.

Nasnas

Ogres – Man-Eating Giants

Ogre is the Western name for a man-eating giant, and most
countries have tales to tell about them. One of the most
fearsome Ogres that has stalked the earth seems to have been
the Japanese Oni, for it was said to be incredibly evil both in
appearance and temper. It appeared as a giant-sized human
body, either male or female, and had long pointed teeth like
elephant's tusks. It also had horns on its head and usually
glowed a bright colour, red and blue being the most
common. The female Oni were often called Yamanba, which
means mountain ogress. The Oni were believed to have lived

103

on a place called Oni Island where they organized themselves on almost military lines, and were thought to make frequent raids on the land of human beings.

The following story – of which there are sixty-seven slightly different versions – is told all over Japan, where it is as well known as the story of Hansel and Gretel is here.

There was once a poor family. The father had died long ago and left the mother with three boys, the eldest of whom was eleven. Although the mother worked as hard as she could every day it became impossible to provide enough food to feed them all. Finally she decided to abandon the children in the mountains. She took the three of them as far as she could. Then, after telling them she was going off to buy sweets, she left them and returned home. The poor children waited and waited and finally the two eldest began to cry. The youngest child, instead of joining in, climbed a tree to see where they were. By then it was pitch dark, but a long way in the distance he could see a tiny light. Urging his brothers to follow him, he set off towards it.

The light was coming from a dilapidated hut where an old woman sat alone beside a large fire. The old woman seemed kind but told them that they must leave the house at once because it belonged to an Oni and when he returned home he would eat them alive. Even as she was speaking, the sound of the Ogre's giant steps could be heard approaching the hut. The old woman flew into a panic, shouting, 'What shall I do, what shall I do?' but before the giant opened the door, she managed to push the children into an underground storage pit, shut the lid and covered it with a mat. The Oni entered the hut with a tremendous clatter, the light glinting on his evil horns and tusks. He began to sniff the air and cried, 'Old woman, humans have been here, I can smell them, I can smell them!' and he started to search the house.

The old woman was very worried and said, 'Just now three boys came by and wanted to stay the night but when they

Ogre

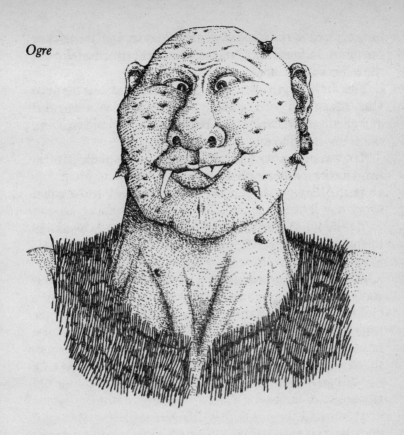

heard you coming they ran away. They must be what you can smell, but they've gone now!'

'If there were children here,' shouted the Oni, 'I must catch them at once.'

He put on his 'Thousand-Ri (3,890 metres, 2,440 miles) in one step' boots and shot out of the door like a bullet. As soon as he had left, the old woman pulled the children out of the pit and told them another road they could take to avoid meeting up with the Oni. The boys ran along for many miles and as they ran they heard the faint sound of thunder. The thunder grew louder and louder with each mile they travelled and eventually it became so loud that they thought they must

105

have arrived at the place where the thunder god lived! They ran around a bend in the road and suddenly discovered what the noise was all about.

There, lying on a bank at the side of the road, was the huge Oni, asleep and snoring loudly! The children were terrified and once again the two eldest boys began to sob and wail, but the youngest child told them to be quiet.

'If we move softly,' he said, 'we can creep by the Oni on tiptoe and he will remain asleep.'

As they quietly slipped by, the younger boy had another idea.

'Surely the Oni is wearing his "Thousand-Ri in one step" boots,' he said. 'If I could get them they would be a great help to us!'

He began to ease the boots off the giant's enormous feet. It was a long and difficult task, as the boots were heavy and the Oni kept tossing and turning in his sleep, but somehow the little boy managed it all alone. He gave the boots to the eldest boy and told him to put them on. He did as he was asked, then strapped the other two children to his back. As he took his first step the three children whistled through the air like the wind.

The Oni awoke and gnashed his teeth in disgust. He set out after the children, but without his boots it was hopeless and he returned home to tell his story to the old woman, who was delighted that the children had escaped. The three boys also returned home, where they worked very hard and helped their mother all they could.

Pegasus, the Winged Horse

The graceful Pegasus, with his beautiful wings, is probably the gentlest, kindest creature in the ancient legends. Pegasus – unlike the Hippogriff, to whom he was related – was a true horse with wings. He was said to have sprung to life after Perseus killed Medusa and dripped her blood on the earth. He plays a vital part in the killing of the hideous Chimera, while taking no part of the glory from Bellerophon.

After killing the Chimera, Bellerophon felt so powerful on the back of the winged horse that he decided to fly up to the top of Mount Olympus on him. Mount Olympus was the home of the gods, and they were extremely angry to see Bellerophon cantering through the sky towards them as though he were a god as well. Zeus, king of the gods, sent a hornet to bite the horse. Poor Pegasus reared up when he was bitten and threw Bellerophon back down to earth with a bump! Pegasus, however, finished the flight to Mount Olympus and was captured by Zeus, who made him pull his thunder-chariot.

The Phoenix

The Phoenix, or bird of the sun, was a mythical Egyptian bird that lived for a thousand years, died and was then reborn. The feathers of the Phoenix were a mixture of red and gold and it had rainbow-coloured wings. Its eyes were sea-blue, its feet were purple. When it flew the sun caught at its brightly coloured plumage and it shimmered and glowed in the sky. It was similar in shape to the eagle but a great deal larger. This mysterious bird lived all alone in a sacred wood in Paradise, where it neither ate nor drank but existed completely on fresh air!

There was never more than one Phoenix at a time. For a thousand years it lived in this Paradise, where there was no grief, hatred or death. As it neared the end of its life-span it began to feel old and tired and, knowing it could never die in this wonderful world of eternal spring, it left, flying westwards across the path of the sun until it came to Arabia, the

land of spices. There it stopped and filled its wings with all
the perfumes and essences it could find – cinnamon, myrrh,
laudanum and many more.

Then it flew on, crossing the desert of Arabia and the
mountains of Syria, until it came to the country that bears its
name, Phoenicia. Choosing one of the tallest palm trees, it
made itself a nest out of the spices it had gathered. At dawn it
awoke and sang a hymn of praise to the rising sun. The voice
of the Phoenix was said to be so beautiful that the sun god
paused for a moment to listen. As he did so, sparks from his
fiery halo set fire to the Phoenix's nest and the bird was

consumed by the flames. Instantly a tiny worm crawled from the ashes of the old Phoenix and began to grow.

In a few days it had grown wings which were strong enough to bear it, and the new baby bird took the ashes of its parent's funeral pyre and flew to Egypt, where it placed them on the altar of the sun temple. As it flew it was joined by hundreds and thousands of other birds, of all shapes and sizes, who were attracted by the wonderful scent it was carrying. After leaving the temple of the sun it flew off eastwards, back to Paradise where it would spend the next thousand years. Its escort of birds flew with it for many hundreds of miles but, when they reached the gates of Paradise, only the Phoenix was allowed to enter and the rest of the birds had to fly down to earth again.

Pookas

Pookas are groups of legendary animals said to haunt the Irish lakes. These creatures usually take the form of an extremely large black dog and occasionally a horse. The Pooka is still used as a bogey to frighten country children to bed. It has given its name to many places in Ireland, such as Lissapuca and Rathpuca. The best-known place is the very deep Poulapuca, or Pooka's Pool, in Wicklow, where the Pooka was widely known for its tendency to waylay unwary travellers at night.

One man, a Mr Martin from Dublin, claimed to have seen the Derry Pooka while on holiday there in 1928. He was fishing in a river that flowed past the end of his garden when he saw a strange creature swimming around the bend towards him. He could not decide what sort of animal it was, but had the strong impression that it was malevolent. He dropped his rod and scrambled up into a tree. The Pooka gazed up at him as it paddled by, baring its teeth in an almost human, slaver-

ing snarl. Its eyes blazed at him fiercely 'like live coals inside the monstrous head'. Mr Martin thought it must have escaped from a zoo, as he could think of no other explanation. When he told local people of his sighting he realized that he had seen the well-known Derry Pooka!

The Remora or Sucking Fish

The queer tales of the sucking fish, or Remora, lasted for many centuries amd were never satisfactorily explained. *Remora* is the Latin word for delay or hindrance. The Greek word for it was *echeneis*, meaning 'stay-ship'. Both words described pretty clearly the Remora's extraordinary behaviour. Apparently it could bring to a halt a large ship under full sail merely by winding its tail round a rock and sucking at the keel of the ship with its mouth – as described in the following poem by Edmund Spenser, *Visions of the World's Vanity*:

Looking far forth into the ocean wide
A goodly ship, with banners bravely delight
And flag in her top-gallant I espied,
Through the main sea making her merry flight.
Fair blew the wind into her bosom right
And the heavens looked lovely all the while
That she did seem to dance, as in delight
And at her own felicity did smile:
All suddenly there clove unto her keel
A little fish that we call remora,
Which stopt her course, and held her by the heel,
That wind nor tide could move her thence away.
Strange thing me seemeth that so small a thing
Should able be so great an one to wring.

The Remora was said to be of 'ashen hue' and had a large disc
on its head which seemed to work in the same way as a very
large rubber suction cup. It was quite small, only 30 centimetres (1 foot) long and as thick as five fingers, but it could
perform incredible feats. One of these sucking fish was said
to have held back Mark Antony's flagship at the Battle of
Actium. Another stopped the Roman Emperor Caligula's
ship in the first century AD, and even though there were four
hundred men straining and sweating over the oars in the
galley, they could not budge it an inch. Later on it was not
only blamed for delaying ships but also delaying the births of
babies!

The Remora Sucking Fish

The Roc

Anyone who has read the adventures of Sindbad the Sailor in *The Arabian Nights* will remember the Roc, the gigantic bird Sindbad met when he was marooned on a desert island. While Sindbad was exploring, he came across a monstrous egg said to be as large as one hundred and forty-eight hens' eggs put together. Sindbad, thinking it must be someone's house, walked around the outside looking for a door. It took him fifty paces to walk all the way around it! While he was doing so, a giant shadow blotted out the sun and, looking up, he saw a bird so enormous that it seemd to fill the sky. The giant egg obviously belonged to it.

Fortunately for the sailor the Roc was kind to him and allowed Sindbad to tie himself to its leg in order to be flown off the island. Sindbad realized how lucky he had been, for he had heard of the Roc before. Apparently it was well known for feeding its young on elephants!

On another of his voyages Sindbad was not quite so lucky. When he and the members of his crew landed again on a deserted island they found another Roc's egg, and in spite of Sindbad's protests the crew insisted on breaking open the huge egg to see what was inside it. When they found a chick, they killed it. This time the Roc was anything but friendly. It fetched its mate and together they dropped giant boulders on Sindbad's ship until it was completely destroyed.

Today the story seems an exciting adventure not to be taken too seriously, but at the time it was written, the Arab sailors and other travellers firmly believed in the Roc. As early as 1376 sailors had described it as a mountain rising into the air. Marco Polo wrote that the bird was so big that it could bear away an elephant in its talons, lift it up to a great height and then let it drop to the ground to be dashed to pieces. The Roc would then swoop down and feed on the carcass. He also reported that the span of its wings reached thirty paces and the wing feathers were twelve paces long. The Roc was said to make its home on the island of Madagascar off the coast of Africa, and it looked very much like an eagle, though a great deal larger.

Although it seems very unlikely that a bird as large as this could have existed, modern research now tells us that many very large birds *did* exist in that part of the world until as late as the seventeenth century. It sounds as if the stories of the Roc, rather than being complete myths, were just exaggerations!

The Salamander

The legendary Salamander of the Middle Ages was said to be a small dragon that actually lived in fire, or a reptile so icy-cold as to be able to put out a fire just by contact. It only ever came out in heavy showers and vanished the minute the rain stopped. Sometimes it was even said that the Salamander was actually recharged by fire and needed it to renew its skin.

All this is rather surprising considering that the Salamander we know today is a small, very timid lizard that makes its home in a cool, damp hole. Like the frog, it prefers to come out in the rain and does not enjoy basking in the sun. The only unusual thing it does is to squirt out a milky-white liquid when frightened, quite harmless to man but poisonous to other small animals that might try to eat it.

The Salamander of long ago, however, was thought to be very poisonous to man, so poisonous in fact that if it crawled up a tree the fruit would be filled with its deadly venom. In the time of Alexander the Great four thousand men and two thousand horses of his mighty army were said to have died after drinking from a stream in India that had also been used by a Salamander. If the milky liquid it squirted should fall upon a man, his skin would be horribly diseased and his hair would fall out. The description of this condition sounds to us today almost like radiation poisoning.

Garments made from the skin of the Salamander were said to be fireproof, and when asbestos was discovered it was supposed to be made from the Salamander's breath.

The reputation of the Salamander as a fierce little beast obviously built up rapidly and shows how folklore can turn one thing into another. Francis I of France adopted the Salamander as his own special mascot, and the little dragon surrounded by licking flames can still be seen in the Fontainebleau palace and many other palaces he built during his reign.

Salamander

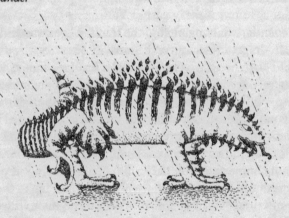

The Sasquatch

For a hundred years now a strange and frightening legend has been related in the remote mountainous regions of North Western America. It tells of monstrous creatures that stride about on two legs like men. Many people claim to have seen them, and tell of giant, ape-like people that leave behind

114

enormous footprints, often as long as 40 centimetres (16 inches). In Canada they are usually called the Sasquatch, an English version of the American Indian name. In the United States they are called 'Bigfoot'.

A newspaper editor from British Columbia, John Green, had collected more than two hundred and fifty reports of sightings, photographs of footprints and other evidence by 1970, covering a vast area from Alaska to Mexico and from the Pacific Coast to Northern Michigan. In the beginning he found the story of the Sasquatch so outrageous and amusing that he couldn't help but become involved in it. As more and more evidence came to light, however, he became a firm believer.

On 30 June 1884 the *Daily British Colonist*, a newspaper published in Victoria, British Columbia, reported that the crew of a train travelling east of Vancouver found what they took to be a man lying next to the track. The train was halted and the man, or whatever he was, brought on board. He turned out to be a very unusual creature, half-man and half-beast. His whole body, except for his hands and feet, was covered with dark glossy hair and he apparently possessed exceptional strength. The creature, christened Jacko by the railway crew, was put on exhibition at Yale University, and in fact there were people as recently as 1946 who remembered seeing him there. No one seems to know what has happened to him since.

As a result of this newspaper report a woman revealed that in 1871, as a seventeen-year-old American-Indian girl from Fort Douglas, she had been kidnapped by a Sasquatch and forced by him to swim the Harrison River. He carried her to a rock shelter where his aged parents lived and, although he looked after her well, he kept her prisoner for a year before taking her home again. This woman continued to tell people her story until she died in 1940, an old lady of eighty-six.

In 1924 a tough lumberjack called Albert Ostman, looking for gold in British Columbia, told of his meeting with the

Sasquatch. Ostman was fast asleep on the ground when a giant two-legged thing lifted him up, sleeping-bag and all, and threw him over his shoulder like a sack of flour. Ostman claimed that, paralysed by fear, he was carried over rough land for about three hours before the kidnapper stopped and dropped him to the ground. By then it was dawn and the terrified lumberjack looked up to see a whole circle of these unlikely animals standing looking at him and talking in a language he did not understand. Remembering the Indian stories of the Sasquatch that he had never previously believed, he now realized suddenly just who his captors were. He described them as being a cross between men and apes. They held Ostman prisoner for six days until one of them swallowed the tin of snuff that Ostman was carrying in his pocket. The poor creature became violently sick, and in the resulting confusion the lumberjack was able to escape.

Again in 1924, this time in Washington State, four prospectors reported that a gang of ape-men had tried to invade their cabin by hurling themselves at the door and the walls and throwing giant boulders on to the roof. They accompanied all this violence by continual screaming and wailing. A posse of policemen and reporters who came to see the cabin later found it very badly damaged indeed. The most frightening thing, however, was the hundreds of giant footprints all around it. The region became known as Ape Canyon and many people have since reported seeing ape-like creatures in that area. What is even more disturbing is that several men have disappeared without a trace!

Other, more concrete evidence has been found over the years, mainly in the form of animal hair and droppings. Scientists who examined the glossy hair say that it comes from no animal known in the world today. The droppings, the same size as human droppings, contain the hair of rats and mice and the remains of vegetables.

Canadians have dozens of eerie Sasquatch stories to tell. These are usually centred on the mysterious Nahanni Valley, located at the southern end of the Mackenzie Mountains. The Indian tribes in that area have avoided the Nahanni Valley since the time of their forefathers. To both natives and settlers this forbidding place is known as 'The Valley of Headless Men'. More than a dozen bold trappers looking for good-quality furs have been found with the flesh stripped from their bones and their heads missing. The search parties have often found the deep indentations of giant human-like feet around the decapitated skeletons.

This, however, is all circumstantial evidence, if of an uncomfortable kind. The largest piece of watertight evidence, a Sasquatch body, has never yet been found.

The most exciting testimony appeared in 1967 when a Washington rancher, Roger Patterson, produced a 16 mm colour film of the Bigfoot. Patterson was another relentless pursuer of this elusive creature. In October 1967 he heard rumours of fresh Bigfoot tracks in Bluff Creek in Northern California. He set off to search the area with his friend, animal tracker Bob Gunlin. They rode together for a week and a half without seeing a single footprint and were ready to return home when, for no apparent reason, Patterson's horse stopped dead in its tracks, snorted wildly and reared up. Something had certainly startled it, and Patterson soon spotted what it was. The enormous hairy creature was about 35 metres (125 feet) away and looked much more human than he had imagined, with a large forehead and wide nostrils. It was completely covered in brown shaggy hair about 10 centimetres (4 inches) long.

Patterson grabbed his ciné-camera from his saddlebag and trotted after it, taking pictures as he went. The creature seemed quite unconcerned and, at one point, turned and stared into the camera with apparent interest. Eventually it walked towards the woods and disappeared. Patterson had plaster casts made of ten of the creature's huge footprints and these were examined by an expert, who pronounced them genuine. He also added that the animal who made them must have weighed 250–300 kilograms (40–50 stone) – nearly one third of a tonne. Patterson's film was shown to scientists but most of them branded it a fake.

A few are open-minded about it, remembering how many scientists refused to admit that there was a giant panda or a giant squid until they came face to face with one! After all, the Bigfoot has 388,000 square kilometres (150,000 square miles) of rugged country as his kingdom, including large areas of forest land that have never been properly penetrated. In this sort of wilderness a cunning animal could easily remain out of sight of man for many years to come.

Satyrs

Satyrs are gods or demons of the forest who are usually associated with fertility rites. The Greeks called them Satyrs but the Romans called them Fauns, Pans and Sylvans. Pictures of Satyrs usually show them as having the hindquarters of a goat and a human body, head and arms. They are thickly covered with dark, curling hair and have short horns on their heads. They also have pointed animal-like ears and hooked noses. They were supposed to live on the three islands of Satirides, somewhere near India, where they inhabited underground caves, rushing out to frighten sailors who happened to land on their island. They used to enjoy pouncing on nymphs, dancing and playing the flute, and were well known for their drunkenness. Many country people used to offer them the first fruits of their harvest and even sacrificed lambs in their honour.

There are many kinds of Satyr, apart from the goat variety. There are those with only one eye and no nose, others with no face who breathe through their chest, and some who have ears so large they can cover their body with them. There are even some in Ethiopia who have only one gigantic foot, which they use as a sunshade when the weather is hot!

Scylla and Charybdis

Scylla and Charybdis were two fearsome sea monsters of Greek legend who sat on either side of the Straits of Messina, a narrow stretch of water that separates the toe of Italy from the island of Sicily. Scylla sat on the Italian shore, Charybdis on the Sicilian shore, and together they destroyed any ships that came within grappling distance.

Charybdis

Scylla was not always a monster; she was once a carefree nymph with whom Glaucus, one of the sea gods, fell desperately in love. However, Glaucus in his turn was loved by Circe. In a fit of jealous rage Circe poured poisonous herbs into the fountain where the nymph always bathed. This turned poor Scylla into a most unlovable creature with twelve feet, six heads, and three rows of teeth. Her twelve legs were permanently surrounded by a pack of growling, snapping dogs. Scylla was so terrified by her new body that she threw herself into the Messina Strait and there, with an eerie yelp like a tortured puppy, devoured numerous sailors whose ships came within reach of her long writhing necks.

Charybdis, on the other side, took the form of a whirlpool and spent her days crouching under a fig tree on the opposite shore. Three times a day she went to the sea and swallowed all the water, then three times a day she vomited it back up again, often wrecking passing ships and drowning their crews. Whichever side of the shore you sailed on in legendary times, the Messina Strait was certainly a very dangerous place to be.

Sea Serpents

In these modern days almost all the solid part of the earth has been thoroughly explored, mapped and photographed, and the highest peaks have been scaled. Our knowledge of the upper air is so great that we can now put men on the moon. Yet the sea, which covers so much of the earth's surface, still keeps most of its mystery. Anything could be hidden there – whole cities or palaces, dragons or sea monsters, you can never be sure of anything with the sea! Possibly its greatest mystery, which over the centuries has stirred everybody's imagination, is the reported sightings of strange sea creatures looking very like gigantic serpents.

It is difficult, of course, to know the truth about the Sea Serpent, as fables and exaggeration have been woven into the stories over the years so that no one really knows where the truth begins. The earliest reported Sea Serpents must have included animals like sharks, seals and whales. However, because of their lack of knowledge, the people who lived long ago were filled with a great suspicion and dread of such creatures. Scandinavian writers, however, often wrote about sea monsters that looked like gigantic snakes and one man described a monster that was 60 metres (200 feet) long and 6 metres (20 feet) round, with a mane 60 centimetres (2 feet) long. He said it was covered with scales, had fiery eyes, and rose up out of the sea like a mast, occasionally snapping up men from the decks of ships. Another writer said that around Norway there was a great snake 60 metres (200 feet) long that sometimes, when the weather was very calm, coiled around great ships, sunk them and devoured their crew. Norwegian fishermen trembled every time they went out to sea.

No one really took these reports seriously, however, until the well-known missionary Bishop Hans Egede claimed to have seen, off the coast of Norway, a monster serpent with a tail as long as the ship he was sailing in. Its head, the bishop tells us, was on a level with the ship's mainmast. It had a long sharp snout and blew water out like a whale. It had broad flippers and a scaly body as wide as the bishop's ship.

From this time onwards, in the newspapers of countries on both sides of the Atlantic, there was a sudden rush of eye-witness reports of Sea Serpents. In 1808 great excitement was caused in Britain when such a monster was found stranded on the Orkney Islands. It was 17 metres (56 feet) long and seemed to answer the usual description of a Sea Serpent. When pieces of its backbone were sent to museums, however, it was revealed as a mere 'basking shark' – but certainly on the large side!

This seemed to put an end to Sea Serpent reports until the summer of 1871, when eleven eye-witnesses swore on oath

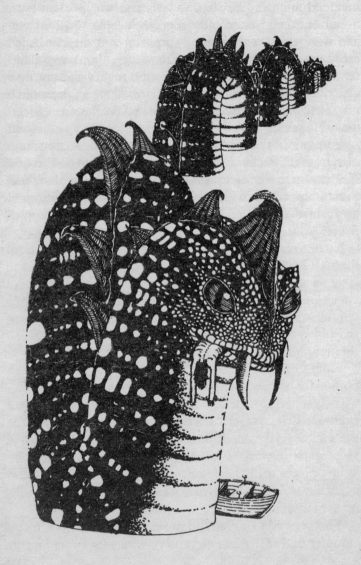

that they had seen one near Cape Anne in Massachusetts. In the investigation that followed the eye-witnesses agreed that the serpent was about 18 metres (60 feet) and moved like a caterpillar. Apart from that, they didn't seem to agree on anything. Some said it was dark brown and white, and others said just dark brown. Its head was compared with the head of a rattlesnake, turtle or serpent. One of the witnesses said it had fins, one said it hadn't and two didn't know. In spite of this there is certainly no doubt that they all saw something pretty frightening.

In the years that followed, serpents were seen regularly off the Norwegian coast. Most of them had pointed heads, large glaring eyes and many humps, and they always moved through the water in a snake-like manner. The Sea Serpent that created the biggest stir in Britain was the one sighted by the officers aboard the British ship HMS *Daedalus*, between the Cape of Good Hope and St Helena, in the early nineteenth century. One day in August, when the weather was dark and cloudy, a midshipman reported that something very unusual was approaching the ship from before the beam. When some of the officers went to have a look they saw an enormous Sea Serpent with its head and shoulders about 110 centimetres (four feet) above the surface of the sea. It was about 18 metres (60 feet) long and travelling at about 24 kilometres (15 miles) an hour. It ignored them completely and seemed in rather a hurry to get somewhere. Several officers and crew watched it for twenty minutes through binoculars, and it made no attempt to dive under the sea or avoid them in any way at all. It was dark brown with a yellowish-white throat. It had no fins, but something like the mane of a horse floated about on its back. The ship's captain, McQuhae, entered this weird happening in the ship's log and had sketches made of what they had seen to take back to London with them.

When Captain McQuhae told of the Sea Serpent they had seen, many other seafaring men came forward to give accounts of Sea Serpents they, too, had seen in oceans from one end of the world to the other. By now almost everyone was ready to believe that the giant Sea Serpent really existed. Zoologists tried to explain away the sightings. Perhaps they could be large seals, a pair of basking sharks one behind the other, a line of porpoises swimming along in single file or even a large mass of floating seaweed. People who had actually seen a Sea Serpent disagreed violently, and as the discussions raged almost every day someone, somewhere, was being frightened by a Sea Serpent.

Over the last hundred years Sea Serpents have been gradually reported less and less. Perhaps people are tired of the amusement and disbelief that greets their stories of strange sightings, perhaps it is just because zoologists keep insisting that no such thing could possibly exist. It certainly does seem strange that no bones or other remains have ever been found in or around the sea. On the other hand, with a sea that covers two-thirds of the globe and in some places descends to a depth of 8 kilometres (5 miles), one can never be sure that in some deep, remote cranny there is not a serpent-like monster living quietly with its family, completely unknown to man.

The Senmurv

One of the descendants of the Griffon was an immortal bird-mammal called the Senmurv, meaning dog-bird. Originating from ancient Persia, it is described as being more bird than mammal and having wings large enough to darken the skies. Later on we see pictures of it with the same wings but with a bird's tail and the head and paws of a dog. In the beginning the Senmurv was a friend to man and lived peacefully in a tree guarded by 99,999 attendants and a magic fish. The seeds of this tree were also magical and could cure all ills.

Whenever the Senmurv landed on the tree its great weight dislodged thousands of seeds, which fell to earth to cure the sick. The Senmurv was also the deadly enemy of snakes (in ancient times any evil or cunning part in folklore was played by a snake or serpent).

The Senmurv was popular in Persian folklore and reappeared much later as the Simurg, a giant bird that made its nest on the highest mountain in Persia. In the eleventh century one of the most popular stories was of the Simurg and a child called Zàl. Zàl was born to King Sàm of Persia with a head of pure white hair. This was considered to be an evil omen by the King's advisers, and they told the King to get rid of him.

Sàm took the tiny baby to the foot of the mountains and sadly left him to die. The Simurg happened to be flying by looking for food for its own baby birds when it heard the wailing of the infant prince. It picked him up and put him with its own fledglings in its nest, where it continued to feed him and care for him until he grew to manhood. Apart from home comforts, it also educated him and taught him how to hunt. Back at the palace, Sàm had never stopped mourning the death of his baby son and often dreamed about the boy. One day he returned to the mountains and prayed for the return of his child. The Simurg heard his prayers and knew it was time for the boy to go back to his father. Zàl was very sad, because he had come to love the Simurg and the other birds very dearly. The Simurg had also grown very fond of Zàl and gave him a wing feather, telling him to throw it on the fire if he was ever in trouble and needed the bird's help.

Zàl went back to his father, became a great warrior, and eventually got married. When his wife was about to give birth to her first child, she became desperately ill and Zàl was told she would die. He threw the Simurg's feather on the fire and soon the sky darkened with the wings of an enormous bird. The Simurg saved the woman's life and she bore Zàl a son who became famous as Rustram the Giant.

Birds with a similar appearance to the Simurg were written about in Russia and the Caucasus. They had names like the Sinam, Simargl and Simyr. They all appear to be related to the original Senmurv and were all basically good-natured and kind.

Serpents and Great Snakes

The Serpent family has never been a popular one, as most humans and animals find snakes unnatural and frightening reptiles. They move in a soft gliding way utterly different from the way two-legged and four-legged animals move, and their strong, hypnotic stare is said to hold their victim rooted to the ground. Snakes, in fact, are no more intelligent than any other animal, but throughout history they have been credited with great wisdom and cunning.

In the opening pages of the Bible, the Devil takes the shape of the Serpent who came to persuade Eve to eat an apple from the wrong tree. In doing so, she gave up her chance of everlasting life. The crafty Serpent ate an apple from the right tree, the Tree of Life, and now, instead of dying every year, renews his youth by shedding his skin and growing a new one underneath. Probably due to this gift of eternal youth, the serpent was often thought to be a healer. In Europe a snake's horn was said to cure any known disease, while in Egypt large live snakes were actually carried to the house of the sick person. Even today, twisted serpents are the symbol of healing and medicine.

There was, however, another, darker side to the serpent's family, and for many centuries it was believed that snakes could cause death merely by breathing on people. Even as recently as 1735 a man was described as having sudden, terrible pain whilst crossing a desert. The cause of the pain, apparently, was a snake which had been watching him from several yards away. The man did not die as he was carrying something called a bezoar, which had the power to cure the effect of all poisons. A bezoar was said to be made of the solid tears of a red deer after it had been bitten by a snake, and was used until the eighteenth century. Other people believed that prevention was better than cure and carried herbs like bay leaves and cardamom, which serpents loathed. Vultures' feathers were also said to be useful, provided you set fire to them when the serpent approached. If you had painted your body with juniper juice before setting out, you would be even more secure! Other people just carried the roots of wild carrot and wild bugloss, which apparently worked just as well.

Every country has its own serpent stories, often about serpents about 1½ kilometres (1 mile) long that crept out of their holes under cover of darkness and devoured entire villages in the twinkling of an eye. Some serpents were said to be so evil that even after they were dead their bodies could poison rivers for many years. There was a snake in China called the White Snake of Hangchow which was supposed to be responsible for causing endless disasters. This was an extremely wicked snake that lived for thousands of years in a mountain cave, worshipping the sun and the moon and planning ways of bringing disaster to the city of Hangchow.

One day she changed her body into that of a woman and went to live in Hangchow. She fell unexpectedly in love with a young man, forgot her evil ways and married him. They were very happy until the day of the Festival of the Poisonous Creatures, which is held every year on the fifth day of the fifth month. A special wine is prepared on that day to weaken the power of five kinds of poisonous creature – the lizard, the centipede, the snake, the frog and the scorpion. The snake-woman foolishly drank some of it and because it weakened her magic powers she changed back into a snake in front of her husband's eyes. He leapt up in terror and rushed off to a temple to seek refuge from her. The snake-woman followed him there, but he refused to return to her and a battle took place between the snake's evil powers and the temple priest's good powers. The priest almost won in that he managed to get the spirit of the white snake into a box, but he could not kill her. The box was buried at the water's edge and the priest warned that great care should be taken of it, for if the water dropped below a certain level the Serpent could escape. He also said that if a general who had conquered three provinces should ever march into Hangchow, the box would open and the Serpent would be set free for ever.

The people who live in Hangchow believe that on the day in 1931 when a general answering the priest's description did march into Hangchow, the snake was set free. They say that this is why soon afterwards the Japanese invaded Manchuria, which was to cause war and poverty not only in China but in many other parts of the world.

THE EIGHT-FORKED SERPENT

A popular story in Japanese mythology is the tale of the Eight-Forked Serpent. This incredible reptile had eight heads and eight tails, and its length extended over eight valleys and eight hills. Moss and pine trees covered its back and pine trees grew on each of its heads. Its sixteen eyes glowed a fiery red. For seven years this monster had devoured seven of the king's lovely young daughters, and in this eighth year was about to devour his youngest and last. The princess was saved by a god called 'Brave-Swift-Impetuous-Male', who filled eight great vats with rice beer and put them where the monster would find them. The Serpent drank the beer greedily and fell into a deep sleep, during which the god cut off the eight heads, causing a river of blood to flow. The number eight is a magic number in Japan, meaning 'many'.

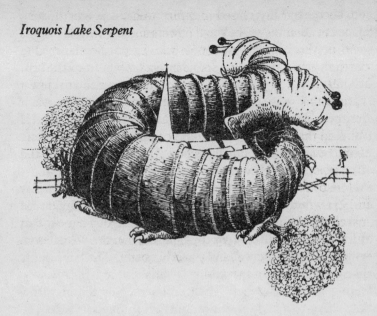

THE IROQUOIS LAKE SERPENT

Serpent stories are common in Iroquois folklore, and most of them are connected with the thunder gods. The most famous serpent story, which can be told in many different ways, is the following one about the Canandaigua Lake Serpent.

A woman lived with her son near a village called Senecas. One day he caught a tiny two-headed Serpent called Kaistowanea and brought him home. First of all the boy placed him in a dark box and fed him with birds and meat. After ten years, however, the Serpent had become so large that it had to sleep on the roof beams of the house. The boy, now grown into a brave warrior, had to go out and hunt deer and bears in order to satisfy the monster's hunger. After a while the Serpent, not satisfied with the food the young man brought him, left the house and went to live on top of a hill near a lake. The Serpent lived there for thirty years, by which time he had become really enormous. He was still a very hungry Serpent and now, with a very large stomach to fill, he cast his eyes on the people who lived below in the village. One morning at daybreak the Serpent came down from the hill, uprooting the trees that stood in his way and making a tremendous noise. He was so large that he could make a complete circle round the village and prevent the villagers from leaving. Some tried to squeeze past him and through the gates, but all found it impossible. The Serpent kept in the same position for several days, and the people began to get more and more distressed and panic-stricken. Finally, in a desperate bid to escape, the villagers banded together and rushed through the gate. They went straight down the throat of the monster. The only people now left in the village were two orphaned children, a boy and his sister. The boy, seeing that the monster's appetite was satisfied and that he was feeling sleepy, somehow managed to creep up to him with a bow and arrow and, carefully aiming it through its scales, he managed to shoot the monster through its heart. The Serpent lurched away from the village and back to the lake, where he died and turned to stone.

The Shaggy Beast

During the Middle Ages a monster lurked on the banks of a quiet stream, the Huisne, in France. Those who saw it said that it was the size of a bull, had the head of a snake and a round, green, furry body. It had feet like a platypus and a reptilian tail that could kill men and animals with ease. As if this was not terrifying enough, it could also shoot out flames that withered crops and could fire stingers out from its fur that killed on impact. At night it raided the stables of the French farmers looking for food, and when they chased after it the monster hid in the Huisne, causing the river to overflow and flood the whole valley. This nasty Shaggy Beast had an appetite for innocent, pure and beautiful things, particularly maidens and children, and would lie in wait until one came along that was to its liking. One day its eye fell on a pretty young girl who happened to be passing its hiding-place; it pounced on her and took her back to its den on the bed of the river. This time it had chosen the wrong girl, for her sweetheart was a fierce warrior who followed the beast and sliced off its tail. Without this powerful weapon the Shaggy Beast could not exist and it died at once. Its death brought great rejoicing to the people.

Shaggy Beast

The Sphinx

Sphinxes have been carved in many shapes and sizes, but basically there are two sorts. The Egyptian Sphinx is the older of the two; it has a lion's body and the head of a man, with shoulder-length straight hair. It usually has a serpent, or uraeus, an Egyptian sign of royalty, wound around its forehead and it can often be found in a horizontal position lying outside temples and tombs. The Greek Sphinx, on the other hand, is definitely feminine, with a woman's head and breasts, the body of a lion and the wings of a bird.

Early Assyrian Sphinxes were male and bearded, but after the seventh century BC, female ones with wings were built. In Phoenicia, Sphinxes were both male and female. As far as we know, no one has ever believed that the Sphinx was a real monster. It seemed to be just a symbol, but obviously a symbol of something rather important, as so many were built. The oldest Sphinxes, probably in Mesopotamia, go back at least five thousand years, but no one has ever discovered who built them first or why. The most likely theory is that they were symbols of death. Certainly no important Egyptian tomb has ever been built without Sphinxes being somewhere around.

The most famous Sphinx of all is the Great Sphinx of Giza. This vast stone beast has lain in the sand, guarding the entrance to the Nile valley, for at least five thousand years. Built in the shape of a man-lion, it is 52 metres (189 feet) long and carved completely out of rock. Despite its enormous size it has been in danger of being lost under the great quantities of sand that are always being blown against it. Occasionally over the thousands of years attempts have been made to clear it, but for most of the time it has been neglected and buried almost up to its chin.

There is a story dating back to 144 BC, about the Sphinx

and its sandy problem. One day, Thothmes IV, just before he became King, was hunting near the giant Sphinx when the sun became very hot. He did as he had often done and lay down to rest in the cool shadow of the stone beast. He had a very vivid dream in which the Sphinx appeared to be struggling in the sand, trying to rid itself of the heavy burden of sand that almost covered it. Its mouth was only just visible but it cried out to Thothmes to free it from the sand that was almost suffocating it.

Thothmes was so impressed by the dream that, as soon as he became King, he had the statue completely swept of sand and built a temple between its enormous paws with a tablet of stone inside telling the story of his dream. This particular Sphinx is the one everyone knows, probably because it has been photographed and discussed so often. The lack of knowledge about it and its inscrutable expression has made it a symbol of all that is mysterious to people all over the world.

There is another interesting Sphinx, not quite so well known but equally mysterious, the Sphinx of Thebes or the Sphinx of the Riddle. This Greek Sphinx was, of course, female and lay crouched on a rock beside the only main road to Thebes. No one remembers how she arrived there but she was decidedly unpopular, as she asked the passers-by riddles. When they could not answer them she devoured them or tossed them over a cliff. The local people found this inconvenient, to say the least, until Oedipus, the King's son, passed along the road. The Sphinx asked him this riddle: 'Which animal walks on four legs in the morning, two legs at noon and three in the evening?'

Oedipus, clever and resourceful, replied, 'Man – for a baby crawls on all fours; when he grows up he walks on two legs and when he is old he walks with a stick.' This must have been the correct answer, for the Sphinx threw *herself* over the precipice!

The Squonk

The saddest beast we have heard about so far is the Squonk. As he lives only in the hemlock forests of Pennsylvania, very few people know about him. His grief seems mainly to be caused by the ugliness of his skin, which is said to be ill-fitting and covered with warts and moles. The only way to trap a Squonk is by following his tear-stained trail. This is particularly successful on very frosty nights, when the tears freeze and sparkle in the moonlight and the Squonk can't move around too quickly. In fact you can actually hear him weeping under the hemlock trees.

One man thought he had captured the Squonk after he lured him into a sack by mimicking his cry. On his way home the man felt his burden get gradually lighter and the sobbing ceased. When he opened the sack all he could find were tears and bubbles.

Squonk

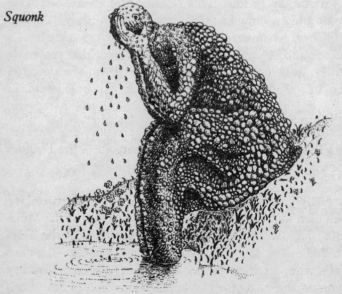

T'ao T'ien or Monster Face

The T'ao T'ien of China was often used in friezes on cere-monial bronzes as far back as 1400 BC, probably just to drive away evil spirits. The beginning of the monster face is lost in time and the only reference to it in early books says that the T'ao T'ien was one of four monsters sent into the outer darkness by the Emperor Shun at about 2000 BC.

The T'ao T'ien is certainly a horrible sight; its monstrous head is connected to one body on the right and another on the left. Usually it has six legs and the front pair is used for both bodies. Its face, more often seen without its body, can be a Dragon's, a tiger's or a man's and is often called an 'Ogre's mask'. The word *T'ao T'ien* actually means 'greedy glutton' and the Chinese paint his face on their dishes to warn them-selves against eating too much.

The Tengu

In long-ago Japan the Tengu claimed to own the whole of the earth. A race of monsters, half-man, half-bird, they had gigantic claws and wings and red beaks. Their eyes were so ferocious and glittering that one glance in your direction felt like a flash of lightning. The first appearance of the Tengu is in one of the classic stories of Japanese history.

For many years there had been a running battle between the Tiara clan and the Minamatos clan. The chief of the Mina-matos, Kiyomon, had already killed the chief of the Tiara clan and swore to kill every one of his children. The dead chief's wife, terrified for her son's safety, offered to marry Kiyomon and bring the two families together, to put an end to the bloodshed. They were married but Kiyomon's wife was only allowed to keep her son Yoshitsune alive provided he was brought up in the women's part of the palace, where he could not learn how to fight or use self-defence. Yoshitsune's mother, however, could not forget how her husband had died and whenever she was alone with her son she talked about it to him, explaining why they were guarded so carefully in the palace.

When he was old enough, Yoshitsune was sent to a monastery, but he never forgot what his mother had told him and he spent all his spare moments rushing into the woods and practising sword-fighting with his shadow. He swore to get revenge for his father's death. One evening on his way back to the monastery he had to take shelter in a valley from a heavy thunderstorm. After a very loud clap of thunder and a flash of lightning he saw in front of him a monstrous figure, like nothing he had ever seen before. It was the King of the Tengu. When Yoshitsune asked him who he was he told him that he had been watching him for many months and admired his determination. As the Tengu tribe were experts at the art of sword-fighting, they decided that they would like to help Yoshitsune. From then on the King of the Tengu gave Yoshitsune lessons every day until he was seventeen and a very good sword-fighter.

Yoshitsune then gathered around him friends of his father who had gone into hiding, and together they battled with the Tiaras and finally defeated them. It would appear from the story that the Tengu were friends to the underdog, but according to the Japanese this was not so. The Tengu were just troublemakers whose pet hate was Buddhism and whose favourite pastime was setting fire to the Buddhist temples and destroying them. This was done purely out of jealousy, as they desperately desired to be worshipped in the same way that Buddha was.

Belief in the Tengu still exists in Japan, but they are no longer said to threaten the Buddhist religion. They are now merely sharp-eyed bird spirits who dwell in quiet corners of Japan in gold-roofed palaces. If a mortal man should visit them there he will be graciously entertained for a time, but usually during the course of the evening the palace and the Tengu disappear, leaving the traveller sitting bewildered on the side of a hill. Their name is a household word in Japan; a wild party is called a 'tengu' party and any story that is likely to be untrue is called a 'tengu rumour'. In fact, you can add the word 'tengu' to anything with a hint of mischief or deceit.

T'ien Kou – the Dog of Heaven

The T'ien Kou, or Celestial Dog as he was sometimes called, was a fearful creature. He was an ill omen that brought only death and destruction and for his food he ate only innocent children. Chinese legend tells us that his main purpose in life was to devour the sun in order to leave the world permanently in the dark. A very nasty monster indeed, he was also called the 'Demon of the Eclipse'.

The heavenly dog did not come to earth very often, which was fortunate, because, when he did, he always caused a great deal of trouble. He appeared for the first time in China in the sixth century BC, enveloped in so many flames that the light from them shone over thousands of miles and poisoned all the crops in the area it shone on. The Emperor of China at that time was terrified of the monster (who was so large that he covered many acres) and to keep him at bay fed him on the livers of human beings. The people of the city were extremely angry and frightened of losing their lives, so they shut themselves in their houses until the monster had gone away.

The T'ien Kou usually appeared in the shape of a great shooting star or meteor, and the only thing to be said in his favour is that there was only one T'ien Kou at a time, which cannot be said for every monster you might meet! Until quite recently he was still feared in remote parts of China as being an evil spirit who ate or kidnapped children.

The Unicorn

There are probably more legends and stories told about the Unicorn than any other mythical animal. Belief in the Unicorn stretches back into the mists of time, but the most amazing stories were written about him in the romance tales of the Middle Ages. At that time European people believed just as strongly in the Unicorn as they did in the elephant and the panther, two other mysterious animals that they had been told about but never had the opportunity to see. The Unicorn had the body of a sleek white horse, the legs and hooves of an antelope and a tail like a lion. Its most remarkable feature was its single twisted horn, which was said to be 110 centimetres (4 feet) long with a white base, black middle and red tip. The horn was so amazingly strong that whatever it pushed against was easily torn to pieces. It was also said to be impossible for any hunter to capture the Unicorn alive. There is one tale of the Unicorn that describes it as being so enormous that it could not enter Noah's Ark during the flood, and yet another story that tells how the Unicorn did enter the Ark but, inexplicably, was thrown out and drowned.

This strong, fierce beast was said to have only one weakness that could lead to its capture. A young girl wearing a garland of flowers would be told by the hunter to sit under a tree and wait there. The Unicorn would always rush out wildly from its lair until it saw the intruder was a young maiden. As if all its strength were sapped just by gazing at her, it would then lie at her feet and put its head in her lap and follow her wherever she led it. She led it, of course, to the waiting hunter, who killed it.

Chinese fables of the Unicorn said that, although it lived

alone on the edge of the world, it would materialize like a
fairy godmother when the King of the country was in
trouble. The Chinese Unicorn was thought to be kind and
gentle, with a voice like a peal of monastery bells. When the
Mongolian leader Genghis Khan took a raiding party of
warriors through the mountain passes of the Hindu Kush, a
Unicorn appeared and bowed its head three times in Genghis
Khan's direction. The terrified soldiers turned tail immediately and marched home again.

A Unicorn's horn, or alicorn, was said to have been found
in 1577 on an island in Frobisher's Strait, and one was also
said to be in the keeping of Queen Elizabeth I. In 1641 a

French marquis said he saw a Unicorn's horn in the Tower of London estimated at £40,000 (a million pounds in today's money) and even tiny slivers of Unicorn's horn were apparently sold at very high prices. This was probably because the horn was used to detect poison in food and drink and give protection from deadly diseases. There was so much concern about whether one was buying a real or false horn that someone actually gave tips in an old recipe book on how to know the real thing:

'For experience of the unicorn's horn, to know whether it be right or not, put silk upon coal, and upon silk the aforesaid horn, and if so be that it be true, the silk will be not a whit consumed.'

An alicorn can still be seen in the Wellcome Museum of Medical History in London. As no real unicorn was ever found, a lot of people must have made a fortune from selling rhinoceros horn and other similar substitutes!

There was supposed to be great rivalry between the Unicorn and the lion for the title of King of Beasts – hence the well-known nursery rhyme:

The lion and the unicorn
Were fighting for the crown
The lion chased the unicorn
All around the town.

The last story we hear is how the Unicorn, chasing the lion, buries its horn in a tree and is completely stuck. The lion leaps on it and kills it.

The Vampire

Throughout the whole shadowy world of monsters, dragons and demons there is no figure so dreaded and loathed and yet wrapped in such a terrible fascination as the Vampire. The name is steeped in folk superstition and every country it the world has stories to tell about him, although he himself belongs to no world at all. According to these legends, the true Vampire is never quite alive nor quite dead. He is something horribly in-between called 'undead', which is a spine-chilling thought! Unlike the rest of the monsters in this book, his appearance is that of a completely normal human being; in fact, he could even be your next-door neighbour. He can stay 'alive', however, only by biting his victims, usually on the neck, and draining their blood.

Early belief in the Vampire is rooted somewhere at the beginning of time and is probably based merely on fear of the unknown. Over the years, stories of vampirism grew more and more familiar – first in Assyria and then in the forests of Mexico. The people of India, China and Malaya came to dread him and Arabian tales tell us of the evil Vampires who gobble up unhappy travellers at crossroads. Even very recently people in remoter parts of Europe like Transylvania and the islands and mountains of Greece have been known to put to death men or women accused of being Vampires. At the beginning of the eighteenth century in Czechoslovakia, reports of vampirism became so widespread that it seemed almost like an epidemic! People all over the world talked about it and read about it and made sure that their doors were firmly bolted when they went to bed at night. The thing that really brought vampirism to the notice of the people in Britain was a novel written by the Irish author Bram Stoker in 1897. It was called *Dracula* and since the day it was published has been in such demand that it has never been allowed to go out of print. Several films have been made of the book, and all have been astonishingly successful.

Vampires in Western legend were usually said to live in Transylvania, a pretty province of Romania near the Hungarian border. Dracula himself lived in Transylvania in a castle 280 metres (1,000 feet) up on a sheer precipice. At the time the book was written, it awoke a great interest in

Vampires and a very great fear of them! Vampires are creatures of the night who, because they are 'undead', are destined to roam the dark hours searching for victims. At cock-crow they must return to their coffins or they will dissolve in the first ray of sunshine, and it must be their own coffin – nobody else's will do!

There are many theories to explain the universal Vampire myth. Yet all cultures, however primitive, recognize that blood is the vital fluid of life. To lose one's vital fluid is to lose one's mortality. This knowledge would stimulate fear in all primitive cultures and the imaginative creation of blood-drinking monsters can be easily explained. While Vampires

Vampire

of less-developed cultures are startlingly demon-like in appearance, the European variety differs not one whit in personal appearance from his victims. Male Vampires in particular have a handsome sophistication that would guarantee them an invitation to the very best parties.

It is said that there are many ways of becoming a Vampire, which vary from country to country. Here is a list, however, that seems to be common to many countries. You are liable to turn into a Vampire if you are one of the following!

1 People who commit suicide;
2 Witches;
3 The seventh son of a seventh son;
4 People who tell lies;
5 Children who haven't been baptized;
6 Criminals;
7 A child born of a mother who has been looked at by a vampire;
8 A dead person whose coffin has been jumped over by a cat or stepped over by a nun or on which a man's shadow has fallen;
9 People who don't eat garlic;
10 Those who have eaten the meat of a sheep that was killed by a wolf;
11 Children who are born on the days of the Church's greatest festivals, for example Christmas Day, Easter Day, etc;
12 Those who have lived an evil life.

The Vampire, in spite of his normal human appearance, was said to be able to transform himself into a dog, snake or bat as the mood took him. If he needed to make a swift escape the shape of a wolf could also come in very useful.

There are few ways of recognizing a Vampire, apart from the fact that he casts no shadow and shows no reflection in a mirror. Vampires meet only once a year, on St Andrew's Eve, when they all get together to plan their evil doings for the following year. The places to avoid when Vampires are about are old ruins, churchyards and crossroads at sundown. In the days when Vampire superstition was at its height, special curfew bells would be rung in remote villages so that no one would leave their homes between sunset and sunrise. People used to spend the nights in large groups telling stories by candlelight. These were the brave ones; the ones who were really scared moved into the towns, where the Vampire never dared to venture.

Vampires were also unable to cross running water, and would never pass through windows and doors rubbed with garlic. The villagers would also spread the paths to the village with the thorns of wild roses so that the Vampire would need to pick up each one before reaching the village. One way of frightening a Vampire away was by showing him a large black dog, preferably with an extra set of eyes painted on top of its head. Why it should frighten him no one knows, but many villagers kept dogs painted like that.

If a Vampire was known to be on the rampage in a particular area, there was one certain way of finding him. A young girl would be mounted on a horse and sent to the local churchyard. The girl had to ride the horse over every grave in the cemetery, and if the horse refused to step over one, that obviously housed the coffin of the sleeping Vampire.

Actually getting rid of the Vampire was quite a difficult job, for in order to transport him from his undead state into a peaceful and final sleep, all the following methods had to be used:

1 A wooden stake made from aspen or hawthorn wood must be driven through the Vampire's heart or navel;
2 Small stones or grains of incense must be placed in the coffin so that the Vampire had something to nibble if he awoke, to delay him leaving the coffin;
3 Garlic must be stuffed in his mouth;
4 Millet seed must be scattered over the Vampire's body, for he could not leave the tomb until every grain had been counted;
5 The Vampire's body must be buried face downwards;
6 Wild, thorny roses must be strung outside the coffin in order to hinder the Vampire's progress from the grave.

There are other legendary ways of killing a Vampire, like shooting him with a silver bullet or burning his coffin so that he cannot return to it. It was important to seek out the local Vampire, according to Romanian tradition, for if he managed to get into the belfry of the village church he would stand aloft in it and read out the names of the people in the village. As their name is called each person in turn drops dead (probably from fright!).

For some strange reason, garlic seems to be the best weapon against Vampires, for they are unable to bear the smell of it. As the Vampire is such an unholy creature he can also be destroyed by sprinkling him with holy water or by waving a crucifix at him, or anything else shaped like a cross.

In South America there really is a Vampire. It is a small bat which does, in fact, live on blood. It is not as sinister as it sounds, as it is a very small creature that bites cows and licks their wounds. It has rarely been known to attack humans, and if it did would be much more likely to bite them on the big toe rather than the neck!

The Werewolf

Another monster probably as ancient and as terrifying as the Vampire is the Werewolf, a man who is transformed into a wolf at every full moon. It bears similarities to the Vampire in that it is a creature of the night that regains its natural form at daybreak. The stories of men who turn into wolves were known in ancient Roman times, which makes them at least two thousand years old. There are examples of Werewolf stories from all parts of the world, from African folk tales to legends of the American Indians. Today, however, the most likely place to find the Werewolf, like the Vampire, seems to be South-Eastern Europe. Obviously the belief tends to remain strong in the places where there are plenty of wolves around.

Although the wolf in legend is thought to be a wicked animal that kills merely for pleasure, in fact real-life wolves are very respectable animals, devoted to their families! They kill only when their cubs are hungry and almost never attack humans. The wolf is now in danger of extinction in many parts of the world, and people are beginning to say that this inoffensive creature does not deserve its bad reputation. It was not always so. Hundreds of years ago, when there were a great many more wolves than there are now, they were not at all peaceful or fearful of humans. They travelled in large packs and hunted by night, killing or maiming the most harmless of animals – usually animals that humans were tending for their own food supplies. When wolves catch animals they devour every single bit of them and leave only the bones. This sort of behaviour pattern brought fear and hatred to country folk, and in early English the word 'wolf' was used to describe the Devil. All over Europe the wolf came to symbolize storms, disappointment and death. No other animal has been more hated or feared by humans.

The Werewolf in legend feeds on these fears and becomes a wild, vindictive creature that tears men to pieces and laps up their blood. One way of becoming a Werewolf is to be bitten by one. Soon after the bite, the victim goes through a series of strange changes. The index fingers of each hand become extended. The palms of his hands begin to itch and gradually become covered with hair, and an unusual five-pointed mark called a pentagram appears on the Werewolf's body. When the moon is full, however, the change becomes even more dramatic. According to legend, on a night when the wolfs-bane plant is in bloom and the moon is full, the man turns into a wolf. Apparently his superhuman strength makes it impossible to keep him behind bars, and he is able to continue his search for plump human victims. At daybreak the Werewolf changes back into human form and has no

recollection of the previous night's evil deeds. He stays and behaves as a normal human being until the next full moon.

France is a country with many Werewolf legends, and there is one particular medieval story that has often been repeated. It tells of a hunter who was attacked by an enormous wolf which walked on its hind legs. The hunter fought bravely and managed to cut off one of the wolf's forepaws, after which the huge beast ran off howling. He put the paw in his bag and took it home. When he opened the bag he saw with horror that the paw was gradually changing into a human hand that bore a ring he recognized. Frantically he searched the house for his wife, and finally found her bleeding to death from many sword wounds and a severed right wrist. Her hand was completely missing.

There is only one sure way of killing a Werewolf, and that is by shooting him with a silver bullet, preferably made from the silver of a melted crucifix. If the Werewolf is shot at full moon he will return to his human form when he is dead. It is therefore better that the corpse be burned rather than buried. Sometimes it is said that the Werewolf is aware of his beastly actions but is powerless to help himself, and should be pitied rather than hated.

The Wild Beast of Barriesdale

In the parish of Knoydart in Scotland there is a loch which, because of its deep, dark and uninviting waters, is called Loch Hourn (Gaelic for Hell). For many years this loch was

Wild Beast of Barriesdale

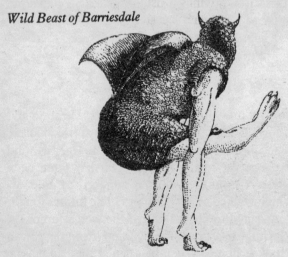

believed to have been haunted by the Wild Beast of Barriesdale.

This strange mammal, which seemed quite at home both on land and in water, had only three legs – two in front and one behind. This, however, did nothing to impede its progress, and it could jump over fences, crofts and even rivers. In 1880 it was observed by a crofter who lived on the shores of Loch Hourn. He described it as a vast three-legged winged creature and claimed that he often saw it flying across the hills of Knoydart. Sometimes it even pursued him as far as his cottage door, but fortunately he had always managed to close it in time!

The Wyvern

Very little is known about the Wyvern or where it came from, but it has been used a great deal on heraldic shields. It looks like a type of flying Serpent, similar to a Dragon, but with two eagle's legs. It does, however, have a barbed Dragon's tail. A Wyvern without wings is usually called a Lindworm. The appearance of a Wyvern was supposed to herald war or an epidemic of a fatal disease like bubonic plague.

Wyvern

The Yale

This heraldic animal, resembling an antelope, is called one of the 'Queen's Beasts'. The Yale is shown on various coats of arms as having the head and body of a horse, a goat's beard and large boar's tusks. It has spots and tufts of hair on its body, cloven hooves and a tufted tail. Its most remarkable feature was its horns, which were large and curving and could be swivelled from back to front entirely at will. It was first portrayed in England in 1440 on the coat of arms of John Beaufort, Duke of Somerset, on his stall plate as Knight of the Garter in St George's Chapel. Before it appeared here it was known in Africa under the name of *eale*. There it was said to be as large as a hippopotamus and had the same remarkable swivelling horns with which to fight off its enemies.

Yale

Aidan Chambers
Haunted Houses £1.25

Shun rooms quiet as the grave, distrust dimly lit silences, and spare an occasional glance over your shoulder as you read these hair-raising tales of ghosts, poltergeists and the supernatural. The most celebrated haunted houses in Britain reveal their secrets – from the ghostly drummer of Cortachy Castle to the visitations at Epworth Parsonage, from the spectral figures of the Garricks's Head to the grinning skulls of Calgarth Hall.

More Haunted Houses 90p

Feel the cold sweat of horror, the icy thrill of dread in these spine-chilling stories of hauntings, mysterious ghosts, unknown sounds and unexplained apparitions. In hundreds of old English houses, ghosts walk the dark passages, striking terror into the hearts of mortals. These are true stories of those ghosts . . .

Great Ghosts of the World £1.25

Feel the fingers of fear creep up your spine as you read these tales of the supernatural. Vampires, devils, ghosts, bunyips, poltergeists – from the ends of the earth come creatures of nightmare to haunt you, taunt you and terrify you . . .

**compiled by Robin Burgess
The Piccolo Bumper Crossword Book: I**

More than 600,000 young crossword fanatics have enjoyed *Piccolo Crossword Books*. Now we have gathered 200 of the very best puzzles into one bumper volume for hours and hours of puzzling pleasure!

The Piccolo Bumper Crossword Book: 2

Improve your word power! Increase your vocabulary! Get the best introduction to the fascinating adult world of crossword puzzles!

Hundreds of thousands of young crossword fanatics have already enjoyed *Piccolo Crossword Books*. Now we have gathered 200 more of the very best puzzles into a second bumper volume to give you hours of fun and puzzling pleasure!

Nigel Blundell and Robin Corry
Nutty News Stories £1.25

Did you hear about the policeman who gave a goldfish the kiss of
life? About the tiddlywinks champs who 'brought the game into
disrepute?' Or about the stolen budgerigar who later 'shopped' the
thief to the police . . . ?

Strange tales turn up every day in the pages of newspapers. Poring
over the files of the world's press, the authors have sought out the
silly, the scintillating and the strange.

This is a book for fans of the fatuous and devotees of dottiness –
people who really appreciate the small lunacies that make everyday
life so exiting . . .

All these books are available at your local bookshop or newsagent,
or can be ordered direct from the publisher. Indicate the number of
copies required and fill in the form below

....

Name ───
(Block letters please)

Address ──

───

Send to CS Department, Pan Books Ltd,
PO Box 40, Basingstoke, Hants .
Please enclose remittance to the value of the cover price plus:
35p for the first book plus 15p per copy for each additional book
ordered to a maximum charge of £1.25 to cover postage and
packing
Applicable only in the UK

While every effort is made to keep prices low, it is sometimes
necessary to increase prices at short notice. Pan Books reserve the
right to show on covers and charge new retail prices which may
differ from those advertised in the text or elsewhere